SACRAMENTO PUBLIC LIBRARY
828 "I" Street
Sacramento, CA 95814
12/14

D0349781

Rethinking
Positive Thinking

CURRENT

Rethinking Positive Thinking

. . . .

Inside the New Science of Motivation

GABRIELE OETTINGEN

Current

CURRENT

Published by the Penguin Group
Penguin Group (USA) LLC
375 Hudson Street
New York, New York 10014

USA | Canada | UK | Ireland | Australia | New Zealand | India | South Africa | China
penguin.com
A Penguin Random House Company

First published by Current, a member of Penguin Group (USA) LLC, 2014

Copyright © 2014 by Gabriele Oettingen
Penguin supports copyright. Copyright fuels creativity, encourages diverse voices, promotes free speech, and creates a vibrant culture. Thank you for buying an authorized edition of this book and for complying with copyright laws by not reproducing, scanning, or distributing any part of it in any form without permission. You are supporting writers and allowing Penguin to continue to publish books for every reader.

Graph on page 70: "Expectancy Effects on Behavior Depend on Self-Regulatory Thought" by Gabriele Oettingen, *Social Cognition*, Vol. 18, 2000, Copyright Guilford Press. Reprinted with permission of The Guilford Press.

LIBRARY OF CONGRESS CATALOGING-IN-PUBLICATION DATA

Oettingen, Gabriele.
Rethinking positive thinking : inside the new science of motivation / Gabriele Oettingen.
pages cm
Includes bibliographical references and index.
ISBN 978-1-59184-687-1 (hardcover)
1. Optimism.   2. Motivation (Psychology)   I. Title.
BF698.35.O57O38 2014
153.8—dc23
2014022172

Printed in the United States of America
1   3   5   7   9   10   8   6   4   2

Set in Sabon
Designed by Spring Hoteling

To Anton, Jakob, and Peter

Contents

Contents

Author's Note

Throughout the book, I draw from the scientific articles and book chapters my colleagues and I have published over the past twenty years. In describing our experiments, our findings, and their implications, I have cited the articles used in the writing of this book so that readers can consult the original texts if they wish. I am deeply cognizant of the rich intellectual contributions of my coauthors, my fellow travelers in the rethinking of positive thinking.

Preface

What is your dearest wish? What dreams do you have for the future? What do you want to be or do? Imagine your dream coming true. How wonderful it would be. How fulfilling.

What holds you back from realizing your wish? What is it in *you* that stops you from really going for it?

Rethinking Positive Thinking is a book about wishes and how to fulfill them. It draws on twenty years of research in the science of motivation. And it presents a single, surprising idea: the obstacles that we think most impede us from realizing our deepest wishes can actually hasten their fulfillment.

Approached by someone who wants to achieve a specific dream, many of us offer simple advice: think positive! Don't dwell on the obstacles, since that will only bring you down; be optimistic, focus on what you want to achieve; imagine a happy future in which you're active and engaged; visualize how much snazzier you'll look when you've lost that twenty pounds, how much happier you'll feel when you've snagged that promotion, how much more attractive your partner will find you when you've quit drinking, how much more successful you'll be when you've started that new business. Channel positive energy and before you know it, all your wishes and goals will come true.

Yet dreamers are not often doers. My research has confirmed that merely dreaming about the future makes people *less* likely to realize their dreams and wishes (as does dwelling on the obstacles in their path). There are multiple reasons why dreaming detached from an awareness of reality doesn't cut it. The pleasurable act of dreaming seems to let us fulfill our wishes in our minds, sapping our energy to perform the hard work of meeting the challenges in real life.

Another way to visualize our future exists, a more complex approach that emerges out of work I've done in the scientific study of human motivation. I call this method "mental contrasting," and it instructs us to dream our dreams but then visualize the personal barriers or impediments that prevent us from achieving these dreams. Perhaps we fear that by bringing our dreams directly up against reality, we'll quash our aspirations—that we'll wind up even more lethargic, unmotivated, and stuck. But that's not what happens. When we perform mental contrasting, we *gain* energy to take action. And when we go on to specify the actions we intend to take as obstacles arise, we energize ourselves even further.

In my studies, people who have applied mental contrasting have become significantly more motivated to quit cigarettes, lose weight, get better grades, sustain healthier relationships, negotiate more effectively in business situations—you name it. Simply put, by adding a bit of realism to people's positive imaginings of the future, mental contrasting enables them to become dreamers *and* doers.

Rethinking Positive Thinking presents scientific research suggesting that starry-eyed dreaming isn't all it's cracked up to be. The book then examines and documents the power of a deceptively simple task: juxtaposing our dreams with the obstacles that prevent their attainment. I delve into why such mental contrasting works, particularly on the level of our subconscious minds, and introduce the specific planning process that renders it even more effective. In the book's last two chapters, I apply the method of mental contrasting to three areas of personal change—becoming healthier, nurturing better relationships, and performing better at school and work—and I offer advice on how to get started with this method in your own life. In particular, I present a four-step procedure based on mental contrasting called WOOP—Wish, Outcome, Obstacle, Plan— that is easy to learn, easy to apply to short- and long-term wishes, and that is scientifically shown to help you become more energized and directed.

I've written *Rethinking Positive Thinking* for individuals who are stuck and don't know what to do about it. It's also for people whose lives are just fine but who might wonder if they could be better. It's for people who have a particular challenge in front of them that they've tried and failed to handle in the past or that they just don't know how to approach. Ultimately, though, I've written it for all of us. We all need help motivating ourselves so that we can stay on track and move ahead.

Why is this? Well, traditional societies have more mechanisms in place—rituals, habits, rules, laws, norms—that circumscribe individual autonomy and assign people roles and responsibilities. The same is true in repressive societies such as North Korea or the former East Germany. When we lack freedom of action, our own choices do not matter so much because external forces push and pull us to act or prevent us from doing so. The challenge people face in these societies primarily involves keeping up their morale and persevering.

Modern Western societies are different, confronting us with what some call the "curse of freedom." The pull and push of tradition and external authority seems to have subsided. Many of us experience more freedom than ever, but we are now required to act on our own—to find it *in us* to stay motivated, energized, engaged, and connected. Nobody is guiding us, day after day, to do what it takes to stay healthy, to pursue a fulfilling career, or to build a family. Nobody is standing over us giving meaning to our lives. It's all on our shoulders. We need to keep ourselves on track—and we need to restore our ability to take constructive action when we get painfully stuck.

Indulging in fantasies about the future doesn't help. Though enjoyable in the short term, fantasies only deplete our efforts and lead us to stumble over and over again. We wind up mired in indecision, on the verge of apathy, prone to an impulsive lurching from action to action, pushed beyond our capabilities, seething with frustration, and falling into an unhappiness we don't understand. But by experiencing our dreams in our minds *and also* grounding ourselves in the realities we are bound to encounter, we can charge ourselves up to tackle life head-on— to connect with what is most real and abiding in our lives.

Whether you are unhappy and struggling with serious problems, or just want to discover, explore, and optimize hidden possibilities and opportunities, this book will deepen your ideas about human motivation and help you boldly chart a path ahead. Like so many participants in my studies, you'll come away more motivated than ever to connect with others, engage with the world around you, and take action. All from a single, counterintuitive question: What holds you back from realizing your dreams?

Rethinking Positive Thinking

Chapter One

. . . .

Dreaming, Not Doing

One of my friends, a man in his early forties whom I'll call Ben, remembers having an intense but rather corny crush on a fellow student when he attended college during the late 1980s. He had seen this woman on several occasions while dining with his friends at a cafeteria on campus. As Ben would shave in the morning or try to pay attention during lectures, his mind would drift and he would picture what it would be like to be in a relationship with this woman. He imagined that she was an artist, and that the two of them would tour architectural ruins in Rome and gaze up at the Sistine Chapel. Maybe she would want to sketch him lying on the quad on a sunny day reading a book, or, better yet, playing jazz piano, as he often did on weekends to earn extra money. Wouldn't it be wonderful to share peaceful moments with someone capable of understanding and sharing his own creativity? For that matter, wouldn't it be wonderful to have a woman to go to the movies with, or to watch a sunset with, or to hop a bus and go to a nearby city with?

Ben didn't tell his friends about his daydreams; he thought of them as his little secret. They were wonderfully satisfying images, but unfortunately, they stayed just that. You see, Ben couldn't bring himself to ask this woman out. He told himself she was a total stranger and he'd make a fool of himself by flirting with her. Besides, he was too busy with schoolwork to date someone. He wanted to get good grades, and it wasn't as if he lacked friends to hang out with on the weekends.

Why didn't Ben have the energy and drive to step up and make his move? He was doing what so many of us regard as essential to success—dreaming about fulfilling our wishes. What was holding him back?

The Cult of Optimism

The notion that simply imagining our deepest wishes coming true will help us attain them is everywhere these days. Bestselling books like *The Secret*[1] and *Chicken Soup for the Soul*[2] teach us that we can make good things happen just by thinking positively, and that positive thinkers are "healthier, more active, more productive—and held in higher regard by those around them."[3] So many of us do think positively, as illustrated by the unvarnished, smiling optimism of contestants on *American Idol*, who speak confidently of their talents and their dream of being discovered, or their counterparts on the *Bachelor*, many of whom express absolute certainty that they will out-shine all the other girls and win the big prize. These individuals gain popularity among audiences not only for having elaborate fantasies about future success, but for living in the bubble of these fantasies and assuming without a sliver of doubt that one day their daydreams will come true.

The cult of optimism goes further than that. Advertising puts forth happy, optimistic people as paragons of success. Politicians at all levels regale the citizenry by claiming the mantle of hope and touting the virtues of the "American dream." Economists chart "consumer confidence" and survey business leaders about how optimistic their outlook is for the future; financial markets rise and fall on such data. Popular music celebrates the ability of dreaming and dreamers to save the world. We're also warned from a young age and at every subsequent turn to rid ourselves of harm-ful "negative self-talk" or to "get out of the hole of negative think-ing" if we want to succeed in life.[4] An inspiring message posted on the wall of a Manhattan middle school exhorts kids to "Reach for the moon; even if you miss, you'll land among the stars."

Optimism appears to prevail even in the face of extreme ad-versity. In 2008, amidst a severe recession, PepsiCo began sur-veying American consumers as part of its Pepsi Optimism Project. In 2010, a full 94 percent of those surveyed felt that "optimism is important in creating new ideas that can have a positive impact on the world." Almost three-quarters of partic-ipants reported that they "expect the best to happen in uncer-tain times." And over 90 percent said that they "believe that optimism can have a strong impact on moving society forward in a positive direction."[5] By 2013, some observers were decry-ing the death of the American dream and American optimism, yet a survey that year sponsored by the Northwestern Mutual

Life Insurance Company found that 73 percent of Americans saw life as "the glass half full" and 79 percent felt that the American dream was still alive.[6] Another poll by Gallup found that 69 percent of those surveyed were "optimistic" about their personal prospects in 2013.[7]

The worship of optimism is not of recent vintage, nor is it uniquely American. It's a theme in world literature, from Marcus Aurelius ("Dwell on the beauty of life")[8] to Samuel Johnson ("that the habit of looking on the best side of everything is worth a thousand a-year")[9] to Dr. Seuss ("And when things start to happen, don't worry, don't stew. Just go right along, you'll start happening too").[10] But Americans traditionally have seemed to relish their optimistic outlook. "Pessimism never won any battle," President Dwight Eisenhower once said. Charlie Chaplin likewise came out on the side of positive thinking, stating that "You'll never find rainbows if you're looking down."[11]

Belief in the power of optimism rests on a simple idea: by looking at the future, we can hang tough and do our best in the present. And if we are going to look ahead, thinking positively seems to be the way to go. What else are we going to do—dwell on how doomed we are to misfortune and misery? How motivating is that? A common adage circulating on the Web (and printed on T-shirts) says it all: "Dream it. Wish it. Do it."

Given optimism's prevalence, it sometimes feels risky to express even mildly negative viewpoints inside institutions and organizations. If you're in the workplace and you take the position of the "realist," others will often label you a "Debby downer" or a killjoy. Filmmakers and television producers often shrink from offering tragic themes and sad endings, fearing that they will come across as "too dark" and turn viewers off. For that matter, what politician wants to question the merit of an optimistic outlook or be seen as breaking from the traditional "can-do" attitude?

As a German citizen who came to the United States relatively late in life, I was initially struck by how much more positive thinking was valued in the United States than back in Europe. In Germany, if you asked how someone was doing, you would usually get a frank answer, such as "I didn't sleep well last night," or "My puppy got sick and it's bothering me." In America, I noticed how people would say, "I'm fine"—even if something was bothering them. I also noticed that people found it jarring when someone violated the unwritten rule of positivity. In 1986, when I was a postdoctoral fellow in Philadelphia, a professor told me about a faculty meeting during which she described some difficult things happening in her life. Her colleagues became highly critical of her for being so "negative" in a professional setting. It was implied that she needed to learn to keep her negativity to herself, so that it wouldn't infect other people.

A Closer Look at Optimism

As unfamiliar as this widespread optimism was to me, I felt thankful for it and did not see it as a counterproductive presence in society. I felt people were being considerate and not dumping all their problems on one another. They valued being in a good mood and keeping others in a good mood as well. I gained a more nuanced perspective, though, when I began to study optimism during the mid-1980s. Initially, I was inspired by what I had seen in East Germany during the Cold War. I researched cross-cultural differences in levels of depressive behavior and compared pessimistic outlooks between individuals living under communism in East Germany with those who lived in West

Germany's more open, democratic society.[12] As part of this research, I went into bars (or *Kneipen*, as Germans call them) in adjacent areas of East and West Berlin to observe and track signs of depression among male bar patrons.[13]

At the time, some people in West Germany and elsewhere wondered whether the communist system held substantial advantages for people's well-being and sense of security. This was a society in which everyone was meant to be equal and cared for by the state, and in which everybody was guaranteed a job and a place to live. However, I found more visible signs of depression—such as slumped postures and sad facial expressions—in patrons of East German bars than I did in patrons of West German bars. I found it fascinating that many people I spoke to in East Germany, just to get through the day, relied on blind optimism and free imagery of a better future.

On one occasion, an East German painter expressed his chagrin at being trapped in East Berlin. He had no canvas, paints, or other supplies required to pursue his art, and on ideological grounds the authorities explicitly discouraged him from doing what he loved most. But this artist, who painted small, appealing figures in the style of Miró and Klee, also told me of his intense dreams of traveling outside of the country to pursue his artistic work. "One day, I'll visit Paris," he said quietly with a smile on his face. Then he turned to gaze out the window and sighed. It was a poignant moment that brought home just how sustaining positive fantasies can be.

Conversations such as this inspired me to refine my understanding of optimism. Martin E. P. Seligman, founder of the positive psychology movement and my research advisor at the University of Pennsylvania in Philadelphia, conceived of optimism as beliefs or expectations about the future that are based on past experiences of success.[14] Seligman found that we are most optimistic when we assess reality as we've known it thus far and logically conclude that the future will likely work out in a similar fashion. If a batter in baseball has already hit .300 with twenty home runs over the past three months of the season, a manager getting ready for a big game will put him in the cleanup position over the player who has hit only .200 with three home runs. Based on experience, the manager believes it more likely that the .300 hitter will get on base in the game—he has a "positive expectation of success."

In East Berlin, though, people I met remained hopeful even though they believed that their wishes for the future very likely *wouldn't* come true. My artist friend had never been to Paris, nor did he have any particular reason based on his past experience to think he would ever visit there. In fact, his past experience suggested he would likely never leave East Germany. Yet still he pictured himself free to pursue his art—painting at all hours, feeling inspired and stimulated and visiting the Louvre. He sustained hope purely on the basis of positive fantasies—free thoughts and images about the future that happened to occur to him and that mentally guided him to and through Paris. His hopefulness amounted to the dreamy anticipation of being surprised given what he knew rationally about his past and the likely grimness of his future reality.

Against this background, Seligman's definition seemed helpful but unable to capture the entire phenomenon of optimism. With his definition the dominant one, many in the discipline seemed to possess an apparent blind spot. Empirical or quantitatively oriented psychologists were hardly writing about or studying positive fantasies or dreams. Influenced by the study of human behavior, they focused on understanding the rational, experience-based judgments people might make about future likelihoods. Expectations were easy to measure and study, while fantasies seemed vague or intangible and thus not suitable for objective analysis. Fantasies also harkened back to Freud,[15] who then (as now) had a reputation for putting forth ideas unsubstantiated by empirical research.

I sensed that positive fantasies were an important part of the human experience, and wanted to explore in depth how they work and affect our behavior. For inspiration, I looked back to the origins of modern psychology—specifically, to the late nineteenth-century thinker William James. In his chapter entitled "The Perception of Reality," in volume two of his seminal work *The Principles of Psychology*, James remarked, "Everyone knows the difference between imagining a thing and believing in its existence, between supposing a proposition and acquiescing in its truth."[16] James was talking about people's outlooks on the past and present, but this distinction also seemed to hold true for the future. It suggested to me that there were in fact two distinct kinds of optimism worth studying: positive expectations that were based on past experience, and the more free-flowing thoughts and images that were rooted in wishes and desires.

I wondered in particular if positive dreams disconnected from past experience would affect people's willingness and ability to take action in their lives. Scholars like Albert Bandura[17] and Martin E. P. Seligman[18] had probed the connection between positive expectations and performance, establishing that expectations increased effort and actual achievement. In their research studies, people who judged their chances of success more favorably based on past experience actually did more to pursue them and achieved their goals more readily. Would fantasizing about something likewise increase the chances of the fantasies actually coming about? Could a flight of fancy, a dream detached from actual experience in the past, energize someone to take action and accomplish the dream?

I thought it probably could. There was no reason to think dreams were any different in their practical impact than expectations; all forms of positive thinking seemed inherently helpful. Wanting to investigate this further, I conducted a study of twenty-five obese women enrolled in a weight-loss program.[19] Before the program began, I asked participants how much weight they wished to lose and how likely it was that they would succeed. Then I asked each participant to complete several short open-ended scenarios. In some they were asked to imagine having successfully completed the program and in others being in situations in which they were tempted to violate their diets.

"You have just completed Penn's weight-loss program," one scenario read. "Tonight you have made plans to go out with an old friend whom you haven't seen in about a year. As you wait for your friend to arrive, you imagine . . ." In another scenario, I asked participants to imagine that they had come upon a plate of doughnuts. What would they think, feel, or do? Asking participants in the study to rate how positive or negative their fantasies seemed to them, I measured whether they dreamed about an idealized outcome of weight loss as well as whether they fantasized about weight loss being an easy process. It was the participants' own, subjective assessment of their dreams—whether *they* found their dreams to be positive or negative—which interested me, not whether I as a researcher happened to think their dreams were positive or negative.[20]

The results of this initial study got my attention. After one year, women who assessed that they were likely to lose weight shed an average of twenty-six pounds more than those who didn't believe they would lose much weight. But here's the kicker. Irrespective of their judgments based on past experience, women who had strong positive fantasies about slimming down—the ones who most positively pictured themselves looking slender and attractive when going out with their friend, or who pictured themselves passing by the doughnuts without batting an eye— lost twenty-four pounds *less* than those who pictured themselves more negatively. Dreaming about achieving a goal apparently didn't help that goal come to fruition. It impeded it from happening. The starry-eyed dreamers in the study were less energized to behave in ways that helped them lose weight.

I published that study back in 1991, and no, it didn't suddenly cause people either in psychology or the wider world to take a more nuanced look at optimism. It didn't do much of anything because the prevailing belief in the power of optimism was just too strong. Almost everyone back then accepted without question the notion that positive views of the future would increase the chances of success. For this reason, some of my colleagues urged me to change course. "Stick closer to established concepts," they told me. "Researching dreams is too risky; it brings you closer to pseudoscience and speculation. If you want people to take you seriously, do research on positive expectations." But I felt research on dreams was meaningful and that my work could contribute to people's lives.

Although my first study was published in a peer-reviewed journal, the second paper I wrote on the subject was rejected several times, with reviewers claiming that the results and arguments were too far-fetched. Some of my peers said they didn't even want to finish reading my paper because my message was ridiculous and even hideous. I was upset and disappointed, but I wanted to see my ideas through.

In science, particular findings must be replicated in order for the scientific community—including me as an author—to accept them. You can't necessarily trust the results of just a few studies. Idiosyncrasies in the data or the analysis could be responsible for the findings. To convince my most skeptical colleagues (and myself) as well as attract a wider audience for my work, I wanted to conduct a number of rigorous, larger studies. I knew I couldn't rest on other people's prior work; the burden was on me to build a painstaking case, putting study after study into place like cinder blocks in a wall until the overall findings were supported.

I got to work, spending twenty years observing people of different ages, in different contexts, in both Germany and the United States. I varied my research methods to anticipate any conceivable objection scholars might have. If I could run studies with all these variations and still come up with a similar result, I would feel confident that I was dealing with a substantial psychological phenomenon. That's exactly what happened.

Again and again, much to my surprise at first, the results turned out to be the same. Positive fantasies, wishes, and dreams detached from an assessment of past experience *didn't* translate into motivation to act toward a more energized, engaged life. It translated into the opposite.

Remember Ben, who dreamed about his mystery woman but never pulled himself away from his studies long enough to ask her out? I investigated whether the positive fantasies of people in his situation did in fact impede them from taking action. I recruited 103 college students who had claimed to have a crush on a member of the opposite sex but who weren't dating that person.[21] I first asked them to assess, on a scale from 0 to 100 percent, how likely it was that they would initiate a relationship with that person (i.e., expectations about the future based on past experiences). Then I asked them to complete a series of hypothetical scenarios related to dating. "You are at a party," one scenario read. "While you are talking to him/her, you see a girl/boy, whom you believe he/she might like, come into the room. As she/he approaches the two of you, you imagine . . ." For each scenario, I asked participants to rate on a 1 (very negative) to 7 (very positive) scale how negative or positive they felt their dream was.

For some students in the sample, such a prompt initiated a positive dream: "The two of us leave the party, everyone watches, especially the other girl. We go outside, sit on a bench, no one around, he puts his arm around me . . . etc. . . ." For others, it elicited a more negative dream: "He and she begin to converse about things which I know nothing about. They seem to be much more comfortable with each other than he and I are, and they don't care very much to involve me in the conversation."

Five months later, I checked in on the students and asked if they had gotten together with the person on whom they had a crush. The results were similar to those obtained in the study of the obese women. The more students expected, based on some reasonable assessment of past experiences, that they would initiate a relationship, the more likely they reported having initiated the relationship. But the more students, like Ben, had indulged in positive fantasies as part of our study, the *less* likely they reported initiating the relationship. Initiating a relationship is a classic challenge requiring motivation and bold action. So is looking for a job. Would job seekers increase their chances of finding employment by positively visualizing themselves acing an interview or sitting in a wonderful new office or handing out flashy new business cards? In 1988, I recruited eighty-three male graduate students at a German university. Most were in their midtwenties. I asked how probable it was that they would find a job, and how much it mattered to them that they be employed. I also asked them to generate and write down any positive fantasies about finding a job and to rate on a scale of 1 (very rarely) to 10 (very often) how often these images entered into their minds. Then I let two years pass before checking back in. The more frequently students had experienced positive fantasies, the *less* success they had. They reported that they sent out fewer applications and received fewer job offers. Ultimately, they reported earning less money. Dreaming about their success hurt them.

Some of the studies mentioned so far—the lovelorn college students, the job seekers—used self-reported data. That is, I assessed the end result by relying on the participants themselves to tell me what happened. What if the participants I was studying got it wrong? What if something about positive fantasies caused them to under- or overreport how much success they were having? That would mess up my results and possibly put my larger findings into question.

I decided to study the phenomenon of positive fantasies in a more objective way, examining the role of optimism in academic achievement. I asked 117 college students in an introductory psychology class what grade they wished to achieve on the midterm, which would happen in two days' time, and how likely they were to achieve it. I measured their fantasies in the usual way—by asking them to complete hypothetical scenarios. "You have already completed your test and today is the day that the grades are posted," one scenario read. "As you are walking toward the building that the board is in, you imagine . . ." One student completed this scenario with a negative fantasy, writing: "What if I messed up the exam? Maybe I should have studied more—where is my grade? Damn—it is a 'C.' How shall I ever make this up?" Others were more positive. I just asked students to rank how positive or negative they thought these fantasies were.

I logged students' midterm and final grades over a six-week period; I didn't rely on the students to report them. As expected, the more students positively fantasized about the grades they would get, the lower they scored and the less they reported studying.

All of my studies to that point involved mostly younger people. I needed to know whether positive fantasies impeded older people from making progress toward their goals as well, so I turned back to the health domain. Arthritis of the hip is one of the most common conditions afflicting older people, with many suffering such terrible pain that they need surgery to replace the affected joint. The disease strikes even the most active of people, severely impeding their lives and sending them into the depths of despair. Recovery differs from patient to patient depending on factors like a patient's age, weight, the presurgical condition of the affected hip, and level of prior activity. For weeks after surgery, patients have to go in for physical therapy and do exercises at home. Little by little, they attempt new movements in their everyday lives—standing, walking, going down stairs, sitting in certain kinds of chairs, riding a recumbent bike, conducting daily chores and activities. The key to a quick and successful recovery is staying as active as possible after surgery without overdoing it, and adapting bodily movements as necessary to relieve strain on the hip.[22]

Wondering if positive fantasies would affect how well patients recovered from hip-replacement surgery, I found fifty-eight patients at a German hospital who were about to undergo their first surgery. I asked them questions about their expectations for recovery—how likely they thought it was that they would be able to walk up stairs and walk with a cane two weeks after surgery and how likely they thought they would be pain free after three months. The patients' answers were based on their assessments of past levels of pain and immobility as well as expectations set for them by doctors based on what they had observed in the past. I also asked patients to imagine themselves after their surgery: waking up in the recovery room, going to buy a newspaper, taking a walk with friends, and performing chores at home.

As in the previous study, participants rated numerically how positive or negative their free thoughts and images were. Two weeks after surgery, with study participants still in the hospital, I checked how far their rehabilitation had proceeded. With the permission of the patients, I got in touch with their physical therapists and asked them to rate on a 1 to 5 scale how well the patients could move their hip joints (range of motion was regarded as a classic indication of a patient's progress after hip-replacement surgery). I also asked therapists how many stairs patients could walk up and down and what their general recovery looked like compared with that of other patients. How much pain were patients experiencing? How strong were their muscles? Did they feel physically well? I chose to consult with physical therapists because they would likely give me an objective and unbiased picture of the patients' progress. These medical professionals knew nothing about my study and its hypothesis. They were simply measuring the patients' angle of motion, ability to go up and down stairs, etc., as part of their normal work.

With the therapists' feedback in hand, I performed statistical analyses of the relationship between the fantasies and outcomes, adjusting for factors such as the patients' weight, gender, and how well their joints functioned before surgery. Yet again I discovered that positive fantasies seemed to hold people back from achieving their goals. The more patients expected they would recover well from their hip surgeries based on an understanding of the steps required, the better they could move their hip joints as rated by their physical therapists, the more stairs they could walk, and the better was their general recovery. The more they visualized a quick and easy recovery, the less these signs of recovery were spotted by their physical therapists.

By the late 1990s, results were beginning to pile up. I studied children suffering from chronic gastrointestinal disease, asthma, and cancer. I studied low-income high school dropouts seeking to graduate from a German vocational school. I studied low-income women seeking to get good grades at an American business skills program.[23] In each of these cases, positive fantasies either did not help or significantly hindered individuals from achieving their goals. Any way you sliced it, conventional wisdom in psychology and self-help literature was wrong: positive thinking wasn't always helpful. Yes, sometimes it did help, but when it came in the form of a free-flowing dream—as so much positive thinking does—it impeded people in the long term from moving ahead. People were quite literally dreaming themselves to a standstill.

The Pain of Lost Decades—and Lost Dollars

During the 1990s and early 2000s, when I gave talks presenting my findings, people responded with surprise and a dose of skepticism. "What?!" they said, their ears perking up. "I had assumed positive thinking was always helpful." Yet these audience members didn't grasp the full gravity of the findings. The ability to sustain motivation isn't a trivial matter. The course of an individual's life is determined by the action she takes in the world. When a person indulges in positive fantasies, she hamstrings herself from becoming all she is capable of being. The costs are substantial—and very real. Think of how relieved the obese women in my study would have felt if they had fantasized less and had lost more weight. Or how many more graduate students would have experienced the thrill of finding a good job. Or how much more comfort the recovering hip-replacement patients would have experienced.

In the wake of the Global Recession of 2009,[24] an appreciation of the costs of excessive optimism has finally gone mainstream. The perils of positive thinking now seem readily—and painfully—apparent, at least insofar as they exist on the level of society as a whole. I became curious about the collective effects of positive fantasies, so my collaborator A. Timur Sevincer and I performed a couple of studies using innovative research methods.[25] We performed an analysis of articles in the financial pages of *USA Today* dating from the beginnings of the financial crisis during 2007–2009 using a computer program that finds and extracts words from the text that carry a given meaning.[26] Extracting all words that dealt with the future or that carried a positive valence, as well as all words that were negative or dealt with the past, we created a "future positive" index. We used this index to perform a statistical analysis exploring whether positive thinking in the financial pages correlated with movements in the Dow Jones Industrial Average. Guess what? We found a clear correlation: the more positive newspaper reporting was in a given week, the more the Dow declined in the week and month that followed.

We wanted to see if we could replicate these findings, so we analyzed presidential speeches from 1933 to 2009 using the same method. In particular, we tested to see whether positive thinking in the speeches correlated with "long-term indicators of economic performance." Again we found a clear relationship: the more positive the inaugural address for a given presidential term, the *lower* the GDP and the higher the unemployment rates were in the following presidential term (see fig. 1).

Positive Thinking in Presidential Inaugural Speeches

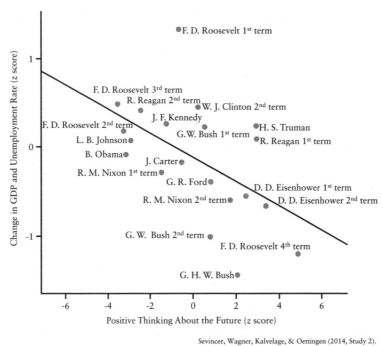

Sevincer, Wagner, Kalvelage, & Oettingen (2014, Study 2). *Psychological Science, 25,* 1010–1017.

Figure 1. The more positive thinking about the future in presidential inaugural speeches, the lower the economic performance in the following terms.

It's hard to fathom the extent to which positive fantasies hinder business performance, and how much economic value is lost as a result, because so few studies in this area have been done. Still, we can speculate that fantasies are extracting a substantial cost. The cultural anthropologist Margaret Mead famously advised that we should "never doubt that a small group of thoughtful, committed citizens can change the world; indeed it's the only thing that ever has."[27] Ask a manager or administrator about this assertion, however, and you'll find quite a bit of doubt. Although valid numbers are hard to come by, it is widely estimated that at least half of all corporate change initiatives fail every year.[28] This factoid has itself become a cliché among consultants and other experts, prompting endless opinionating as to the culprits behind the constant failure of companies to change. In one recent survey of executives, participants cited a handful of reasons, such as "lack of clearly defined and/or achievable milestones and objectives to measure progress," "lack of commitment by senior management," "poor communication," "employee resistance," and "insufficient funding."[29] Innovation initiatives would seem especially hard to execute, judging from a blog posting on the *Huffington Post* that listed no fewer than fifty-six reasons why so many fail.[30]

Or take entrepreneurship. It's known that over 50 percent of all new businesses fail in the first five years,[31] but what about the almost uncountable ideas that never become working businesses due to positive fantasizing? As one senior business consultant reflects: "For some people I've seen, the idea of change does become gratifying in and of itself. Whether it's innovation or a new product idea or a new strategy, the idea sometimes becomes so salient that there is little sense of the execution that might be required to bring it about. It's as if just having the idea will make it happen."[32] Just as in our personal lives, our dreams likely short-circuit our ability to take action in the workplace.

We don't yet know the full economic and social costs of fantasizing, but what we do know is that if you want to succeed economically as a political leader, you may not want to provide a lot of economic happy talk in your inaugural address. If you as a journalist or an analyst want the economy to thrive, you might not want to gloat publicly about how great the outlook is. And if you want to achieve a personal goal such as losing weight, recovering from an illness, getting a job, or landing a hot date, you should think twice about just sitting back and dreaming about it. As a strategy for staying motivated and achieving goals, idealizing the future doesn't work for individuals and it apparently doesn't work so well for large corporations or entire societies either.

That's not to say idealizing the future "dooms" every person to failure. My results speak to statistical likelihoods of success and failure—the chances of moving ahead or staying stuck. Still, likelihoods do matter. Based on two decades of research findings, replicated across a variety of research participants, contexts, and methods, you would be ill-advised to indulge in dreams about achieving your goals and then assume you're well on a path to success. Life just doesn't work that way.

Chapter Two

. . . .

The Upside of Dreaming

So is dreaming entirely detrimental? Should individuals avoid positive fantasies and feel guilty whenever they indulge in them?

Some psychologists, beginning with Sigmund Freud, have suggested precisely that. Freud argued that fantasies could please people temporarily, but that over the long term they impeded personality development and caused anxiety and other neurotic behavior. Humans, Freud thought, turned to fantasies or daydreams to compensate for unpleasant realities, in the process embracing morally questionable and irrational behavior. The solution was to avoid positive fantasy.[1] Neo-Freudians and followers of a school called humanistic psychology picked up on this thinking around the middle of the twentieth century, arguing that only thoughts corresponding to reality, and not fantasies, were "mentally healthy" and capable of leading to self-actualization. As one scholar, Marie Jahoda, put it, ". . . the perception of reality is called mentally healthy when what the individual sees corresponds to what is actually there,"[2] and specifically, when the individual acknowledges elements of herself that she doesn't like very much. The well-known humanistic psychologist Abraham Maslow proclaimed that "healthy individuals find it possible to accept themselves and their own nature without chagrin or complaint"[3]—a position that might be construed as implicitly critical of wishful dreams and fantasies.[4]

Such thinking persists today, and not just in academic psychology. Since the Global Recession of 2009, commentators have come down hard on idealizations and dreams that aren't grounded in "reality." Barbara Ehrenreich's 2009 book *Bright Sided: How the Relentless Promotion of Positive Thinking Has Undermined America* offers a withering critique of what Ehrenreich calls "the mass delusion that is positive thinking." Ehrenreich advocates that we "get outside ourselves and see things 'as they are,' or as uncolored as possible by our own feelings and fantasies. . . ." We need to detach from our emotions and moor ourselves to objective facts, including those we might not like. "Realism—to the point of defensive pessimism—is a prerequisite not only for human survival but for all animal species. Watch almost any wild creature for a few moments and you will be impressed, above all, by its vigilance."[5]

Wild creatures are one thing, college students quite another. Meet Rachel, a twenty-three-year-old recent college graduate living in a New England city. Four years earlier, when she was still in school, she lived through the heartbreaking experience of seeing her boyfriend Tim go to jail for a drug offense. Tim wasn't just any boyfriend; he was the love of Rachel's life (or so it seemed). As she recounts in an unpublished essay, "We fell in love because nothing else made any sense. We fell in love because we needed each other."

Tim's conviction was stunning because he hadn't been in any kind of trouble before. He wasn't a drug addict or a gangster but a hard worker who had run circles around Rachel at the hardware store where they had first met and held jobs. "Tim felt useless if he wasn't being productive or doing something to keep busy," Rachel recalls. "He always worked." Unfortunately, the recession hit Tim's family hard. He had to start paying his own way, including chipping in for college tuition. No matter how many hours he put in at his part-time jobs, he couldn't earn all the money he needed. So he turned to selling a little pot on the side.

"Tim could be defined by many terms," Rachel reflects, "worker, lover, fighter, son, employee, boyfriend, best friend, but I never, in my wildest dreams, imagined he would voluntarily add 'pot dealer' to the list. But he did." He sold marijuana for a couple of months, as did several other young people in their town. When Rachel tried to stop him, Tim pleaded that she didn't know what it was like to experience extreme financial hardship. He was right—Rachel's family was more affluent—but Rachel argued that drugs were inherently bad. Tim wouldn't listen, so she relented, crossing her fingers that Tim would quickly make the money he needed and then get out of the business before he got into any trouble. She didn't agree with his actions, but could understand his point of view and didn't love him any less.

Tim did get out of the business and months passed. But

then, with no warning, the police swooped in and arrested him three days after his nineteenth birthday. During his final transaction, Tim had gotten caught in a sting operation. The cops had him on tape selling drugs to an informant. Although it was his first offense, the judge came down hard, sentencing him to six months in jail as well as three years' probation.

Still desperately in love, Rachel felt obligated to stand by Tim's side. She was terrified to appear with him at his sentencing, afraid of the shame she'd feel and of seeing his family members in pain, but skipping it wasn't an option. In an exchange of e-mails, I asked her how she made it through the anxious and depressing days of waiting before the sentencing. It turns out that positive fantasies played a vital role. "I daydreamed that the judge or the prosecutor was saying something terrible about Tim, just a nasty comment, and then I would jump up and say, 'Hey! You don't know him *personally*! He's a good person at heart; he just made a mistake!' And then his mom would stand up and talk about him as a baby and his friends would stand up and talk about him as a teenager. . . . Together, we would create this giant team of persuasion and the judge would be so overwhelmed by our love and compassion for this *supposed* convict that he would let Tim go and condemn the police officers who so wrongly arrested him."

All people experience situations in which they perceive there is nothing they can do about their circumstances and must simply wait for something to happen. Some of these situations, like Rachel's, are merely uncomfortable, while others amount to life or death. Either way, when the point is not to take purposeful action but rather to hang tight and passively "stay in the game," positive fantasies can prove useful, even essential. There are other ways in which positive fantasies help, too. They can provide individuals with short-term pleasure, and they enable people to imaginatively explore options for future action. Positive fantasies comprise a vital and useful part of life—just not in the ways people usually think. What are they good for? Not everything, but certainly not nothing. It depends on the situation.

I Have a Dream

If you stop to think about it, many people who lack control over their lives have endured by imagining idealized outcomes. Some of these free-flowing dreams may seem exaggerated and unrealistic, but they are sustaining nonetheless. My East German friend visualized a trip to Paris in order to obtain what a political system had denied him—a chance to express ideas and emotions in paint. Women in abusive relationships will frequently endure their daily lives by fantasizing—and even believing—that one day their husbands will change. A clergyman I know of whose thirty-year-old son is a quadriplegic said that he frequently gets through the day by fantasizing about new technology that will allow his son to walk again.[6]

In his famous "I Have a Dream" speech,[7] Martin Luther King Jr. acknowledged that "the manacles of segregation and the chains of discrimination" still oppressed American blacks, and that "the Negro is still languished in the corners of American society and finds himself an exile in his own land." But King urges his audience not to "wallow in the valley of despair." He affirms that he has a positive fantasy, a dream, and he ends his speech by elaborating on the notion that one day "freedom will ring" and "*all* of God's children, black men and white men, Jews and Gentiles, Protestants and Catholics, will be able to join hands and sing in the words of the old Negro spiritual: *Free at last! Free at last! Thank God Almighty, we are free at last!*"

Another startling example of how positive fantasies enable perseverance comes from Nazi concentration camps. Starvation was rife in the camps, and inmates regularly perished because of it. In the words of one survivor: "We have a calendar in Birkenau. It is hunger. . . . Morning is hunger. Afternoon is hunger. Evening is hunger."[8] Yet some of the inmates dealt with hunger by doing something almost unimaginable: collecting favorite recipes into cookbooks. Created in a camp called Terezin, one hand-sewn cookbook contained recipes for dishes like chocolate cake, macaroons, farina dumplings, and potato salad. Michael Berenbaum, director of the United States Holocaust Research Institute, regards the recalling of old recipes as "an act of discipline that required [inmates] to suppress their current hunger and to think of the ordinary world before the camps—and perhaps to dare to dream of a world after the camps."[9] Others placed more emphasis on the fantasy aspect of saving recipes and arguing over ingredients. As one survivor of the camp put it, writing the recipes ". . . was a dream and I think it gave them, in a way, strength to survive it."[10]

How precisely do dreams help when people lack the capacity to act? Let's consider where positive fantasies come from. Early on in my research, I suspected that positive fantasies arise from physiological or psychological needs. To test that hypothesis, my collaborator Heather Barry Kappes and I recruited a group of seventy undergraduate students and asked them not to eat or drink for a period of four hours before the start of the study.[11] Arriving at the laboratory, students answered questions designed to measure how thirsty they were. We then offered each of them a number of foods, including dry, salty crackers.

We included the crackers specifically, since they are known to increase thirst. Some of the students were given water to drink to quench their thirst, while others weren't. Members of both groups were then asked to fantasize an ending to the following scenario: "You're in a restaurant and the waitress brings you a big glass of ice water. You pick up the cup and drink the water . . ." We also elicited fantasies unrelated to the participants' thirst by asking them to complete a scenario in which a friend asks them whether joining a gym was a good idea. We had participants rate on numeric scales how positive and negative, respectively, their fantasies were and we also had an independent judge do the same.

Under our hypothesis, the thirstier students would fantasize more positively about having water to drink than the less thirsty students. And that's exactly what happened. The need to drink spawned positive thoughts and images about satisfying that need.

Thirst is a "basic physiological need," as conceptualized by theorists like Abraham Maslow,[12] in contrast to higher-order needs, such as safety, belonging, esteem, and self-actualization. More recent researchers have identified other higher-order needs, such as the need to feel competent, autonomous as an individual, and capable of relating to others.[13] I wondered if people who experienced different kinds of higher-order needs would also tend to fantasize more positively about filling these needs.

One higher-level need we can all identify with is having a meaning or purpose in life. How happy or fulfilled can we be without a reason to get up in the morning? Heather Barry Kappes and I found eighty-five adults in the waiting rooms of various government offices in a large German city. We had everyone peruse a paragraph titled "What Gives Life Meaning?" The paragraph stated that work makes us who we are and tends to give rise to meaning in life. Yet we gave out slightly different versions of the paragraph. Half of the participants, all randomly chosen, received a paragraph intended to arouse the need for a purpose in life. The other half of the participants simply read a text that implicitly affirmed that people lead meaningful lives.

As in previous studies, we then prompted fantasies by having the participants complete different scenarios. In this case, one scenario read as follows: "You are sitting in a company's reception area waiting for an interview for a position that you're interested in. The interviewer comes out, shakes your hand, and leads you to the office to begin the interview . . ." We had participants rate how positive or negative their fantasies were. Some participants came forward with highly positive fantasies such as "I'm extremely motivated and I'm looking forward to the interview. I have the chance to get my favorite job; that's why I'm so well prepared. And I don't have any anxiety about it." Other fantasies were more negative: "I tell myself absolutely don't do anything wrong. I have to manage this. Always laugh nicely, act natural. Coffee—yes or no? Damn, my application materials are messed up!"

As expected, participants whose sense of finding meaning in life we had challenged fantasized more positively about doing well in the imagined job interview. We replicated these findings in two additional studies, one in which we challenged participants' feelings of connectedness with others (a social need), the other in which we challenged people's sense that they could influence others' behaviors or emotions (another social need). In both cases, individuals with an aroused need tended to fantasize more positively about that need's fulfillment. Our article concluded that needs are "one variable affecting mental travel to a positive future."

If needs give way to positive fantasies, those fantasies should also help us satisfy the underlying needs. When we dream about satisfying our needs, we're paying closer attention to those needs as well as to relevant stimuli that might lead to their satisfaction. As William James observed, "What holds attention determines action."[14] The traveler stranded in the desert fantasizing about water will more likely quench his thirst because he'll be alert to relevant cues that suggest water might be around. Similarly, the clergyman with the quadriplegic son indicated that as a result of his fantasies, he finds himself noticing scientific innovations that might benefit his son while watching the news or surfing the Internet.[15]

There's an important caveat here. While fantasizing might help us satisfy some needs, it doesn't help us fulfill needs that require significant energy, effort, or commitment. We've already seen that just dreaming about positive outcomes doesn't help people realize their dreams. As other research I've done has shown, something about positive fantasies hinders us in handling hard tasks but spurs us to perform easy tasks. If the thirsty man in the desert needs only to stop walking and bend over to drink from a pool of water, savoring positive fantasies will likely help him by enabling him to notice the water and to stay alert and moving while waiting for the pool to appear. But if a person lacks purpose in life and envisions finding one by landing a leading role in a movie opposite Angelina Jolie (an achievement that usually requires, at a minimum, auditioning day after day for months or years), indulging in positive fantasies probably will hinder him in his quest.

Another reason fantasizing helps us passively stay in the game is that it may distract us from the burdensome chore of waiting. Instead of going out of our minds, or veering off into despair, we are able to imagine a pleasant outcome, something we might like to see happen. In Rachel's case, the days before her boyfriend's sentencing were long and worrisome, but imagining the judge being swayed by a mounting chorus of support for her boyfriend kept her from giving up. "I experienced far more patience than I ever thought I had in me," she recalls. In the treatment of post-traumatic stress disorder, it's common for therapists to encourage patients to visualize themselves in a safe place—a pleasant, nurturing environment that engages all their five senses. This imaging technique allows patients to get through the months or even years of therapy that might be required to process and heal the deeper trauma.[16]

These examples involve fairly extraordinary circumstances, but positive fantasies can also help distract us from the chore of waiting in more mundane situations. Gallup's 2013 State of the American Workplace report found that a full 70 percent of American workers "are 'not engaged' or 'actively disengaged' with their jobs."[17] How might they be coping with long, boring, unfulfilling days at work? Jerome Singer,[18] a pioneer in investigating what people do when they zone out during tasks, observed that when tasks don't challenge people and seem to saddle them with boredom, positive thoughts and daydreams make a welcome appearance, allowing them to joyously kill time. Similarly, Eric Klinger[19] points to what he calls "current concerns"—in other words, unfulfilled goals and wishes—that give rise to seemingly random thoughts as we perform tasks in our everyday lives. Sometimes these thoughts help us to endure boredom without causing any problems, but other times they interfere with work and prevent us from performing important chores well.

I invite you to apply the findings in this chapter to your own lives.

As an exercise, think of something that truly is beyond your control, a situation in which you are left waiting with no recourse. Think of a need that is going unfulfilled and that you aren't capable of fulfilling. Maybe you're a law student waiting to find out if you have passed the bar exam. A patient nervous about receiving a test result. A home buyer waiting to see if she has been approved for a mortgage. Sit down for a moment and fantasize about the desired outcome. Really let your mind go. Let the images fly. Imagine the relief you feel learning you've passed the exam or received a clean bill of health. Imagine your girlfriend hugging you. Imagine celebrating that evening over dinner. Imagine the smile of pride on your parents' faces when they walk through your new house. Do you feel any better? Does the time pass any faster? In this situation, dreaming can be an important short-term resource to fall back on, even if our dreams never do wind up coming true.

Many people have asked me if positive fantasies can help us get through a serious disease such as cancer. My initial research doesn't suggest a clear connection between positive fantasies and successful outcomes among cancer patients. If you think about it, many forms of cancer—even those with poor prognoses—have some form of available treatment. Except perhaps for the very end stage of an illness in which a patient is receiving palliative care, there is usually room for action. People with cancer often try all kinds of alternative treatments when the conventional ones don't seem promising, and for the most serious cancers, there's always hope of falling into that small percentage of people who *do* manage to survive. To achieve the best possible outcome, cancer patients must not just "stay in the game"—they must be motivated to take care of themselves and seek aid. Positive fantasies of a recovery are not enough, and they might possibly inhibit helpful action.

A Hit of Pleasure

There is at least one other reason positive fantasies are worthwhile. To understand it, let's stop for a moment to consider a pervasive problem among young people in America today. A 2013 study of over 123,000 college and university students found that at any given time within the previous twelve months, 59.6 percent had felt "very sad," 31.3 percent had felt "so depressed that it was difficult to function," and 45 percent felt "things were hopeless." The vast majority of the interviewed students—83.7 percent—reported feeling "overwhelmed by all they had to do" and 79.1 percent felt "exhausted (not from physical activity)."[20]

My collaborator Doris Mayer and I decided to see if dreaming about an ideal future could help ease depression in young people. We asked eighty-eight students at a large American university to complete a questionnaire that led them to imagine themselves in twelve scenarios.[21] They had to visualize each scenario, play it out in their minds, and write down the resulting dreams. "You're working on an important project," one scenario read. "You know that you cannot meet the deadline and you have asked your client for an extension. You know that it is likely that he will grant you one. Today your client will let you know about his decision. While you are waiting in your office for him to call . . ." We also had students complete a questionnaire that is widely recognized as an effective way of measuring how depressed someone is.

Four weeks later, we checked in on the students and measured their depression levels again using the same questionnaire. We found that the more positive students' fantasies were, the more depressed they had become. However, we also found that dreaming more frequently had corresponded to *less* depression at the time of the dreaming itself. Dreaming about a positive future seemed to protect against sadness in the short term but promote it over the long term. It coincided with a short-term hit of pleasure that ultimately wore off and predicted increased depression.

In its ability to provide short-term relief from depression, dreaming about the future works much like coping mechanisms that help people deal with extreme pain. Thought processes and behaviors such as denying a problem's existence or losing oneself in drinking or other drugs have been shown to engender more depression as time goes on.[22] People fall into passivity and don't actually *do* much about the cause of their pain; over time, it wears on their mood. Yet short-term alleviation of depression is no insignificant thing. Getting people to dream might well be a valuable asset in therapists' toolboxes as a "Band-Aid" solution when people need immediate relief.

Looking beyond depression, we find that positive fantasies are virtually omnipresent in our daily lives—and many would argue happily so. As historians and social theorists have long pointed out, modern consumer culture has sold products and experiences by entrancing people with fantasies of what they could have, be, or do in the future. Luxury car brands like BMW, Mercedes, or Lexus support the fantasy that, by simply sitting in their flashy cars, we can enter a world of taste, prestige, and power. For decades, makers of cleaning and cooking products have appealed to busy women with the fantasy that, by using the product, they will become doting mothers to their children and "good" spouses for their husbands. Similarly, video games offer players the fleeting but pleasurable fantasy that they are a race car driver, secret agent, or professional football player. Corona beer's marketing offers weary, workaday consumers the fantasy of a "vacation in a bottle." By just cracking open the cap and taking a sip, they can imaginatively experience themselves lying on a white beach under a hot sun, flicking their cell phones into the surf, and whiling the time away as they please.

In Touch with Reality

For some, pointing to the fleeting pleasures of dreaming might seem a strange way to argue that dreams have value. Aren't people too hedonistic already and not sober and circumspect enough? As Barbara Ehrenreich suggests, the problem seems to be that we have become so attached to the comforts of positive thinking that we lose our grasp on the external "reality" and compromise our ability to solve pressing social and political problems.

But positive fantasies may actually help you become *more* in tune with what is real, not less. I'm talking about a certain kind of reality here: what you really want. Dreaming is a vital way of claiming what belongs to you, what resonates with you on a deeper, often hidden level. It's also an effective and even critical path to discovering what *isn't* real for you.

Let's say you're a college student heading for medical school. Both your parents are doctors and your aunt is a physician's assistant. In your family, going into the medical profession is just something that you do. You're sitting by yourself one day eating a double cheeseburger when you start dreaming about your future career. You picture yourself as a doctor wearing that bright white jacket with your name monogrammed on the left lapel followed by "M.D." Then you imagine yourself by a patient's bedside, taking her pulse, reviewing her chart, answering her uneasy questions. You're halfway through your cheeseburger at this point, so deep in your dreams that you lose touch with what's going on in the cafeteria around you. You imagine yourself working night shifts in a harshly lit room breathing in hospital smells and typing patient data into the computer. It occurs to you that, actually, you're not a night owl, you don't like harshly lit rooms, and hospital smells make you gag. And as you again visualize yourself by a sick patient's bed, you imagine the patient throwing up all over herself. You think that . . . well, you know, working in a hospital is probably pretty disgusting. Who wants to be around sick people all the time? As you finish the last bites of your cheeseburger, you linger on this thought. You imagine how long and dreary the days are likely to be, how much memorizing you're likely to be doing in medical school, how liberating it will be at the end of a long shift to leave the stuffiness of the hospital and breathe fresh air again.

A lot can change during the time it takes to eat a cheeseburger. But whether or not you change your mind all at once or little by little over months of dreaming, or whether you wind up not changing it at all, vividly imagining a potential future gives you an opportunity to mentally experience what you might do or become, to explore possible choices and assess whether they are right for you. It yields valuable information and prepares you to make the right decision for the future.

Fantasizing is a powerful means of exploration because it allows you a virtual experience of your wishes without requiring that you actually take action and make a commitment. These wishes can unfold in the immediate future—even in the next hour or day of your life. Jeannie, a marketing manager at a large apparel manufacturer, sometimes finds herself sitting in her office fantasizing about what she wishes to accomplish over the next day. Knowing she will be leaving the following evening on an extended business trip, she imagines herself spending the morning packing, talking on the phone with colleagues, and meeting with three of her direct reports to work on their up-coming presentation. As she gazes out her office window, she fantasizes what it will feel like to sit on the airplane knowing she has completed her tasks; she imagines the sense of lightness she'll feel as she sips a cold drink with nothing else to do but skim through a newspaper and gently fall asleep.

But then, as Jeannie clicks idly through her e-mail, she realizes that something is oddly missing. Her son, whom she hasn't seen much recently, is in town and what she *really* wants is to spend time with him. She imagines biking with him to their favorite French bistro for a late breakfast. He orders his usual baguette with jam or maybe the chocolate almond croissant he used to order when he was little, as Jeannie gets a double espresso. They sit there together for a while without talking and then, eventually, as the friendly waiter delivers their food, they become immersed in a conversation about what had happened in their lives during the weeks when they hadn't seen each other. Yes, this is what Jeannie wants. So she changes her wish—and her plans.

Looking more closely at everyday life, one can find many examples of the explorative use of dreaming. When high school students are deciding where to go to college, they typically visit campuses to "get a feel" for what it might be like to go there. During these visits, as prospective students walk around the academic buildings, libraries, and dorms, they typically imagine themselves in these places the following year. They embark on extended positive fantasies about waking up each day in the dorms, eating their meals in the dining hall or at nearby restaurants, going to classes in the ivy-covered buildings, smelling the wood of the staircases as they walk between levels in the library, hanging out on the lawn playing Frisbee or talking to their friends. Returning home from campus visits, students remember their fantasies and may deepen them as they learn about other schools and move toward a final decision. To some extent, this entire process injects a dose of randomness into college selection; if a student happened to visit a certain campus on a cold and rainy day, her fantasies are likely to be significantly different than if she had visited when the weather was merely humid and overcast, or if it was hot and sunny and all the students were hanging out on the arts lawn.

It's common for people to pursue the task of planning their futures in a rational way. They make long lists of what they want to accomplish, sometimes making additional lists of the likely pros and cons attached to each choice. Fantasizing is a different process with advantages of its own. Watching images flow freely in their minds, people let themselves go, and in the process arrive at a comprehensive, intuitive understanding of what they *really* want for themselves, what is essential to their doing and being. They become aware not just of what makes sense, but of what *feels* right.

Just like a good book or movie lets you mentally visit far-away places, you can visit your own possible futures. Who knows what you might discover?

As an exercise, I invite you to find a comfortable spot and identify an important wish. Close your eyes for just a moment and fantasize about fulfilling the wish. How do you see the wish playing out? How are you feeling as it plays out? Who else is in the picture? Try to imagine as many sensory details as possible, going through all the five senses. If your mind begins to wander to other wishes or to negative images related to the original wish, don't fight it. Just go with it and observe the fantasies, suspending all judgment.

Try writing down your fantasies. Set a timer and scribble down the images as they come, paying no attention to grammar or logic (the surrealists, who were very much into dreams, called this "automatic writing"). Or, using your smartphone, try to talk aloud and record your voice. That way, you can go back and listen to the progression of the images floating across your mind. You might find yourself confirming your initial wishes and taking them even further. Or you might find that your dearest wishes are much different than you originally thought, and more exciting than you ever conceived.

Upon completing this exercise, take a moment to reflect. Our positive fantasies *can* take away the worries of today and our immediate suffering. Born of pressing human needs, dreams can help us persevere in difficult situations when we have no control and are forced to wait for our needs to be satisfied from the outside. In less dire situations, they offer us escapist pleasure in the present, and they also help us "keep things real" by enabling us to virtually explore our deeper desires—in other words, what we *really* want, what belongs to us, and what we belong to.

Dreams are good for quite a lot, then—it just depends on the specific context. They might not help us lose more weight, quit smoking, or get a job, but they do help us stay alive in the desert, survive under political repression, and keep the faith as we wait for judges to sentence our weed-dealing boyfriends. The key is simply not to ask more of our fantasies than they can give us. So long as we understand the power and limits of positive fantasies, they can serve us as helpmates, not as restraints. We would be wrong to jettison our dreams, just as we are wrong to blindly assume that simply dreaming something can make it so.

Chapter Three

. . . .

Fooling Our Minds

S o why *don't* positive dreams about the future help us stop smoking, get in better shape, and improve our relationships? What is it about dreaming—as opposed to optimism based on reasonable expectations about the future—that hamstrings people from achieving their wishes? How does dreaming affect us on a cognitive, emotional, and even physiological level?

Heather Barry Kappes and I looked for answers by turning to an unlikely source: women's shoes. Many women spend a significant amount of time fantasizing about their footwear—especially sleek, beautiful heels. Wanting to understand women's fascination for stylish shoes a little better, we recruited 164 female college students.[1] We randomly divided the women into two groups and invited them to fill out questionnaires on a computer. For three minutes, a message on the screen asked the women to imagine themselves all dressed up in fabulous high heels. They were then prompted to jot down their spontaneous thoughts and daydreams. "I am wearing my favorite black patent-leather closed-toe shoes," one woman wrote. "I'm wearing them with a black dress and walking down the street comfortably and confidently. I am able to walk down the street quickly and passersby notice me. They make me feel taller, more sophisticated and more confident. The heels make my legs look longer and thinner."

When the three minutes were up, we asked one group of the students to generate still more positive thoughts about wearing their heels. The other group received the following instructions: "Maybe not everything about these high-heeled shoes is wonderful. Are they really as cool as you thought? Do you look good? Does everyone admire you? Please generate and write down some negative thoughts and daydreams about this condition." This second group of women had little trouble complying, tapping into painful experiences of wearing heels. One woman wrote: "My feet hurt really badly and I trip once or twice while wearing them. Not everyone notices my high heels or even comments on how pretty they are. I feel gawky at times compared to those around me. I want to take them off just to ease the pain they cause and a blister is forming on my right foot."

Before and after the three-minute sessions, we did something few people think to do when indulging in daydreaming: we took systolic blood pressure readings. Systolic blood pressure is a cardiovascular measure that can be taken to reveal how energized or motivated a person is.[2] When we're excited to do something, our bodies take in more oxygen and nutrients;

our cardiovascular systems rise to meet our bodies' needs by pumping more blood.[3] We weren't just interested in examining whether women's shoe fascinations were real or not. We wanted to see if dreaming about shoes would render these women more or less energized. If the mere act of dreaming diminished energy, this would help explain the linkage we had been seeing between dreaming and reduced performance. Perhaps people were losing less weight or making less progress recovering from hip surgery simply because their *dreams* were relaxing them, making it harder for them to get off the couch and move toward their goals.

That is exactly what we found. The women in the two groups did not differ in their blood pressure (averaged across each group) at the outset. But after their imagery exercise, women who had only positively fantasized about wearing high heels showed *lower* systolic blood pressure. By contrast, the women whose positive fantasies we'd quelled by asking them to negatively question their heels showed no change in blood pressure. The women in our study who had positively fantasized for six minutes—just six minutes—walked out of the room less energized than they had been when they'd entered. A cigarette typically produces a rise in blood pressure of about five to ten points (or millimeters of mercury, the official measure).[4] The positive fantasy exercise lowered blood pressure by almost half that much.

It's remarkable that positive fantasies help us relax to such an extent that it shows up in physiological tests. If you want to unwind, you can take some deep breaths, get a massage, or go for a walk—but you can also try simply closing your eyes and fantasizing about some future outcome that you might enjoy. But what about when your objective is to make your wish a reality? The *last* thing you want to be is relaxed. You want to be energized enough to get off the couch and lose those pounds or find that job or study for that test, and you want to be motivated enough to stay engaged even when the inevitable obstacles or challenges arise. We've seen that the principle of "Dream it. Wish it. Do it." does not hold true, and now we know why: in dreaming it, you undercut the energy you need to do it. You put yourself in a temporary state of bliss, calmness—and lethargy.

Unfit for the Hard Stuff

Other research Heather Barry Kappes and I have done has confirmed that positive fantasies make us *especially* unfit to handle hard tasks that require concerted effort. We asked eighty-one college students to read a 2007 *New York Times* article about people in Sierra Leone who suffer from the country's dire shortage of painkillers.[5] Imagine that you have a toothache and need to have a cavity filled. In the United States, you'd never have a moderately painful procedure without novocaine or some other medication to numb the pain. In Sierra Leone, people who suffer excruciating injuries such as third-degree burns or illnesses such as tetanus often lack access to even basic, over-the-counter painkillers.[6]

We asked some of the students to fantasize that the shortage of medication had been remedied; other students were asked simply to recount facts about the resolution of the crisis, without fantasizing. Thereafter students read that an organization called Treatment 4 All was working to help residents of Sierra Leone and needed donations. One group of randomly selected students was asked to give only $1, while students in the other group were asked to give a much more substantial sum of $25.

Those who had positively fantasized that the situation had

been resolved were just as likely to give only $1, but were *less* inclined to give $25 than students in the factual-thought control group. Combining this finding with our previous research, we can surmise that participants who positively fantasized were less energized to surmount the hurdle represented by a larger donation (for today's overworked, debt-ridden students, $25 is a significant amount). In a second study, we asked participants to donate time (five minutes or sixty minutes) instead of money and came up with the same finding.

Likewise, we can speculate whether customers of online daily deal services like Groupon are also affected by positive fantasies. When people buy a Groupon (a coupon redeemable at a local vendor), they likely harbor dreams about enjoying a product or service at a reduced cost. Yet a considerable percentage (21.7 percent) of daily deal customers wind up never redeeming their coupons, perhaps because under the influence of fantasy, the actual logistics of using the product or service by a given date proved too difficult when real life hit.[7]

In other situations, too, our fantasy lives might well be inadvertently stymieing us and "dumbing us down." When we spend two hours fantasizing about car chases in the darkness of a movie theater, do we then become less capable of complex driving tasks? Do teens taking the SATs perform worse after they read a book about a kid who slides easily into Harvard? Are all those political commentators driveling about current events in part hampered by pre–air time fantasies about being vaunted experts in their fields? Toward early afternoon, when people are tired and fantasizing about the promotion they're going to get based on their superior conflict-resolution skills, are they less able to handle a complicated customer service request that comes through? Should heart surgeons, engineers at nuclear power plants, air traffic controllers, and others who undertake complex tasks as a significant part of their daily routine be purposely discouraged from fantasizing about excelling at these tasks? Would employers of these people benefit from educating individuals to avoid indulging in fantasies about their own competence?

Think of a time when you're sitting at your office grinding away at a boring task. Your mind drifts to your lunch break and how enjoyable it would be to eat a delicious chicken shawarma sandwich, with its juicy meat, crunchy fresh vegetables, spicy exotic sauce, and warm fresh bread. Your taste buds salivating, you jump off your chair, run to the elevator, and take it fifteen flights down to the street. As you near the door, you remember that construction workers have blocked the sidewalk and you'll need to take a longer route to the corner café. Instead of delighting in the shawarma, you find yourself once again at the boring old food cart in your building's lobby, unpacking the plastic around a premade sandwich and loathing the stale bread, wilted lettuce, and cheap cold cuts.

Why didn't you go to the trouble to get the shawarma? Now you know: the very positive fantasy that got you distracted from your boring task also drained you of the extra energy you needed to buy the shawarma. You wound up back in your office not having finished your work and, even worse, having gulped down a cold, unsatisfying lunch. Might I suggest that the next time you face a boring task, you don't even come close to indulging in a positive, distracting fantasy; you'll be making a tough situation even worse. Or at the very least, make sure that you fully explore, through your fantasies, what you really want. Maybe what you really desire is to finish the boring task and then give yourself a nice, relaxing lunch as a reward.

Four-Dollar Martinis and Relaxing Train Rides

The shoe study yielded exciting results, but we hadn't conducted any tests to see if positive fantasies prompted people to actually *feel* more relaxed and, further, to see if they actually declined to take action as a result. Setting out to remedy the first of these, Heather Barry Kappes and I recruited fifty undergraduate students.[8] We told them that part of the study was an essay contest with a $200 prize and that, as preparation, the students would perform an exercise to help their writing. The exercise consisted of the usual fantasy prompts. One group of students was asked to positively fantasize that they received the $200 prize and that things went well. They were given an unlimited amount of time to write up their fantasies, as opposed to the three minutes in the shoe study. "The best part about winning this $200 is that I don't have to be so stingy anymore," one student wrote. "I can go out to dinner with friends and be social again. I have had to be so stringent with my spending recently and I have felt more distant from my friends BUT NOW we go to our favorite bar and get drunk off of four-dollar martinis." A worthy fantasy indeed.

As a control, we had a second group of students imagine that they might not win the $200 prize and that everything wouldn't go well. One student wrote: "Two hundred dollars is a lot of money and I could definitely use it and treat myself for once. I am always working; I never have a time to just breathe and relax. I have to pick the prize up either Thursday at 1 or Friday at 1. I cannot pick it up. I have to go to work on Thursday and my internship on Friday. As soon as I believe that things are looking up, my ridiculous schedule does not allow me to accept my prize. I really need this prize. I do not need the money; instead I need the feeling of joy that accompanies good luck." Notice how rambling this response is. As I've mentioned, positive fantasies (and negative ones, too) are free-flowing streams of imagery; they take twists and turns, sometimes doubling back on themselves.

Right after the fantasy exercises, we asked participants to tell us how energized they felt. On a 1 to 5 scale, with one representing "not at all" and five representing "extremely," they indicated whether they felt "excited," "enthusiastic," and "active." Similar to the shoe study, students who had positively fantasized reported feeling significantly less energized than did students who had negatively fantasized.

The question remained: Would students whose energy was diminished by dreaming actually decline to take action? We devised a further experiment to find out. We divided forty-nine undergraduate students into two groups. One group was told to imagine that the upcoming week would be a great one—that everything they did would unfold as they hoped. Students wrote about getting good grades on tests, watching their favorite television programs, having a good time at parties, and taking relaxing train rides home for the weekend. Students in the other group were asked "to generate and write down their thoughts and daydreams about the coming week"—any thoughts or daydreams that might come to mind. "I think that my music quiz will go reasonably well," one participant wrote, "and hopefully I will finish drafting my final paper for my writing class. I am excited that it is the last week of classes for the semester. I have been waiting for summer a long time, and it is very rewarding to finish classes. Hopefully the weather will stay nice; it is quite a motivator. But according to the weather Monday will rain, which would be typical."

As in the last study, we asked students to rate how energized they felt. We also asked them to come back in a week's time and fill out a psychological test designed to measure how well they had mastered the challenges of daily life. This test had questions on it like "How well did the past week go for you?" and "How disappointed do you feel about the way that this past week went for you?" Students also reported if they had felt in control and "on top of their time" during the previous week.

As we expected, students who had been asked to positively fantasize reported feeling less energized than those who had been prompted to give a neutral fantasy. In addition, the less energized students reported feeling, the less they had accomplished during the week in question. Positive fantasies led to lower energy levels, which in turn predicted lower accomplishment. This result is astounding when we keep in mind that we were asking students in the study only to spend a few minutes fantasizing. Yet that alone was enough to deflate their energy and diminish their performance for the following week.

These results correspond well with many people's daily experiences. In the face of a big challenge or chore, people often fantasize about how it feels to have achieved it. In the moment, the fantasy feels good, and it also feels relaxing—so much so that we don't take action.

Try it yourself right now: Set a timer for five minutes, and identify an important wish you have which has been recently on your mind. Imagine having fulfilled the wish, finally having settled your concern. Experience the fulfillment. Let the flow of images wash over you. Write your positive thoughts and images down. When five minutes are up, how do you feel? Do you feel relieved?

Relaxed? Hyped up? If you happen to have a blood pressure cuff, take your blood pressure before and after. And then check in with yourself a few days or a week later. How motivated did you feel to take action to achieve your wish? Did you find yourself sluggish and uninspired? Or did you take any action? If so, how?

On one level, the finding that dreaming lowers our energy and leaves us in a pleasant state of relaxation might seem surprising. What about all those inspirational speakers who spit out visions of a transcendent future and tell us that "we can get there"? Didn't President Barack Obama energize America and the world as a presidential candidate in 2008 with his rousing speeches about "The Audacity of Hope"? Conventional wisdom holds that dreams are supposed to hype us up, not calm us down. But as our data show, that is not usually how it works. Positive fantasies might make us feel electrified for an instant, but at the very least, this feeling does not correspond to what is going on in our bodies and nonconsciously in our minds. More often than not, we are the exact opposite of electrified. It never ceases to impress me that we can measure a decline in energy and motivation almost instantly after a fantasy of wish fulfillment passes through a person's mind.

Mental Attainment

The tendency of our dreams to diminish motivation and action begged the question of what was going on in our minds to bring about increased relaxation. "Realists" are critical of positive fantasies and often point to dreaming as a hedonistic and even sinful pursuit, yet they often haven't gone to the trouble of understanding how dreaming actually works. I had a hypothesis: dreaming about the future operates on a nonconscious level to affect our cognition—that is, how we perceive our world. In dreaming about something, we don't just take delight in an imagined future. As we're dreaming, our minds are fooled into actually thinking we've *attained* that future. As far as our minds are concerned, dreaming becomes a fairly convincing (if short-lived) substitute for doing. We've seen this before; the substitution of dreaming for doing is precisely what enables positive fantasies to help us explore possible futures.

I'm not the first one to explore the idea of what we might call "mental attainment." Back in the eighteenth century, the philosopher David Hume argued something similar when he postulated that imagined sensations can rile us up as much as actual sensations do.[9] During the twentieth century, academic psychologists theorized that fantasy is a kind of behavior on par with action. Research has also borne Hume out, finding that the sheer mental simulation of physical activities caused changes in people's breathing and heart rates, just as actually doing the activities would.[10]

More broadly, it seems clear that our imaginations are powerful enough to have real-life effects. Recent research in psychology has found that repeatedly imagining the act of eating a delicious food reduces our actual consumption of that food (something you might try if you're trying to kick your chocolate habit).[11] Our results likewise suggest that, far from causing something to occur in reality, as many people think, the act of imagining can *stop* something from coming into being. In particular, by fooling our brains into thinking we're already successful, we lose motivation and energy to do what it takes to actually become successful.

In one challenging study, Heather Barry Kappes, Andreas Kappes, and I explored whether positive fantasies fool us into thinking we've attained our dreams.[12] What made this study more complicated than the ones I've presented so far in this book was that we were trying to measure a nonconscious cognitive process. We couldn't just ask participants to tell us if they felt that fantasizing about a wish had allowed them to mentally attain that wish, since that would make them aware of the nonconscious process and thus alter the process. We needed to find a way to observe or measure that nonconscious process directly.

We had a group of undergraduate students read a passage about a character who comes home and catches his partner sleeping with his best friend. We asked the students to imagine that they were this character, and that the events in the story were really happening to them. Then we gave the participants a test in which we showed them—in quick succession—a series of words and word-like collections of letters (e.g., "varrish" or "suilly"). The students had to press a button marked "yes" if the letters before them were a real word and a button marked "no" if they were not. Some of the actual words in the series related to violence (e.g., cruel, fist) while others were unrelated to violence.

We had the same participants read a second part of the story, in which the character took revenge by doing things like leveling a public insult at the best friend who had cheated or damaging the friend's bike. Participants imagined again that they were the character, and then repeated the word task. We also asked them how positive they felt about their fantasies of taking revenge. We devised this experiment to see whether students who had generated more positive fantasies about taking revenge would identify more slowly the words associated with violence or aggression. As other scholars have already shown,[13] when people attain a goal, words associated with the goal become less accessible to the mind; thus, they take longer to identify goal-related words. So the speed with which the students would identify words related to aggression would stand in as a proxy for whether they had mentally attained the goal of getting revenge on their cheating partner and best friend. As we expected, the more positive students' fantasies were about exacting revenge, the slower they were at identifying words relating to violence and aggression, which suggested that they had already attained the goal in their minds.

We can now understand why our dreams so often relax us and sink our performance, no matter how strongly committed we may feel we are to attaining them. As a result of dreaming, our minds tell us that we don't need to exercise or eat right in order to lose weight. We don't need to pound the pavement and show up at interview after interview in search of a job. If we're a corporate leader dreaming of changing the organization, we don't need to bother ourselves with all the hard work of communicating, allocating funding, and coaching managers to implement the change. Our minds have already shot ahead to the end state of success and accomplishment. We relax and enjoy the state of attainment—even though everything in reality still remains to be done. Unknowingly, we become singularly unprepared for the one thing that might allow us to actually achieve success: taking action.

Are We Locked In to Our Dreams?

What makes dreaming even more damaging to staying engaged and moving ahead in life is that it skews how we search for information about the world, leaving us with an imbalanced and possibly unrealistic view. Because our dreams spawn a pleasant, relaxed state in which we perceive that we've already fulfilled our wishes, it seems logical that we'd want to stay in this state for as long as possible and that we'd pay more attention to information that seemed to prolong the fantasy. If through our dreams we virtually experience going on an African safari, we'd look for newspaper articles that depicted the delights of a safari rather than articles that revealed how expensive, dangerous, or unsatisfying a safari is. Over time, we'd come to inhabit a "dream world" of our own making, comprising valid but lopsided information from outside. The nuances and complexity of real life would get lost, and the actual decisions we make would suffer in turn.

To start testing these ideas, Heather Barry Kappes and I went back to where we began: shoes. We invited seventy-seven female students and asked them to answer a series of questions on the computer about how often they intended to wear high-heeled shoes in the coming year and whether they had worn heels in the past year.[14] We didn't want to alert students as to the purpose of the study, so we embedded these questions among others asking how often students anticipated wearing other items like skinny jeans or underwire bras. We then prompted students to fantasize about how amazing it would be to wear a magnificent pair of high-heeled shoes. Three minutes later, students continued to another screen. One group was asked to write down more daydreams about how beautiful these imagined shoes were and how much attention they garnered while wearing them. Another group was asked to generate questioning or negative fantasies about the shoes.

We then had participants look at a constructed website

called Fashion Facts, on the pretext that they'd be offering their opinions about how well written the site was. We made sure that this site contained information both about how great it was to wear high-heeled shoes (e.g., "Women who wear high heels at least three times per week have increased muscle tone in their calves and glutes") and how not-so-great it was (e.g., "Wearing heels might result in unsightly growths on your feet such as corns, calluses, hammertoe, bunions, and 'pump bump'").[15] All in all, the site had ten pages to it, one page each on the pros and cons of five fashion items, including shoes. The students could read only one page at a time, and couldn't read a page more than once. We then measured how long they lingered on each page. As expected, students who had positively fantasized about the shoes spent more time reading about the respective pros than about the cons.

I should note that this effect was not observed in all the students—only in those who didn't strongly intend to actually wear high-heeled shoes. In other words, if you're dreaming about sailing the Caribbean in your own private yacht, and you happen to have a yacht as well as plans to vacation with it in the near future, your information processing will not be skewed. If, however, like most people, you don't have a yacht and it's a real stretch to think you'll soon vacation on one, your information process *is* skewed.

People who positively fantasize about the future—and that's probably all of us—thus put themselves in a double bind. On the one hand, they inadvertently relax and fool their minds into thinking they've attained their wishes. Meanwhile, their dreams lock them cognitively into these same wishes, sustaining their fantasies by avoiding information that might otherwise prompt them to step outside, get some perspective on their wishes, and perhaps resolve to take a different path. The result all too often is frustration, failure, and, at the extreme, a deep-seated feeling of being stuck. We dream of fitting into those skinny jeans, we resolve to lose weight, we sustain our fantasies about how wonderful it would be to look good in the outfit, and then we fail again and again to turn down those supersized orders of fries or make the effort to take a dance class after a long day at the office. We look around, wondering why others seem to be successful at realizing their ambitions—while we're not.

There's an old joke about a man who dreams of hitting it big in the lottery. He dreams of how great his life would be if only he won the multimillion-dollar jackpot. *Oh, all my problems will be solved*, the man thinks. *I'll live in a big mansion, I won't have to worry about my car payments anymore, and I'll be able to buy new clothes.* As the weeks go by, his fantasies deepen. *If I buy the new clothes, I'll look better and be able to get more dates. We'll fly away for weekends in Paris. We'll enjoy tremendous meals at three-star restaurants.* And yet, one month later, two months later, he still hasn't won. He keeps waiting and fantasizing. A year later, no luck. Finally, at the edge of desperation, he prays to God: *Please, God, let me win the lottery. How come you haven't let me? What do you have against me? What have I ever done to you?*

Much to the man's surprise, the clouds part and celestial harps can be heard. There is a brilliant light. In a booming voice, God says in frustration, "Would you buy a ticket already?"

It isn't enough to sit and dream; we have to take action and make sacrifices to buy a ticket in life. Our dreams may be realizable, but they come down to challenges that require engagement and action. The good news, as we'll see, is that it's possible to move energetically toward many of our wishes, and to do a much better job deciding which wishes are worth our effort and which aren't. The solution, affirmed by many other experiments I've done, isn't to do away with dreaming and positive thinking. Rather, it's making the most of our fantasies by brushing them up against the very thing most of us are taught to ignore or diminish: the obstacles that stand in our way.

Chapter Four

. . . .

The Wise Pursuit of Our Dreams

Let's take a few moments to try an exercise we haven't done yet. Pick a quiet spot and get comfortable. Take out a sheet of paper and a pen. Now answer this question: What is your most important wish for the next week involving your relationships with others or your work life?

Maybe your husband has asked you to go to dinner this weekend at his college friend's house. You had an argument with this friend a few months earlier and haven't spoken since. You really want to apologize and reconcile.

Maybe your boss applauded you six months earlier for doing a great job on a project. She intimated at the time that you deserved a raise, but you had your annual performance review and the raise didn't come. Meanwhile, a colleague of yours who hadn't been performing so well got a raise. You'd like to broach the issue with your boss and hopefully figure out how to get that raise after all.

Or perhaps your firm has an exciting business opportunity with a new client, one that would boost the entire firm's revenues by 25 percent. Someone has to make the final pitch before the client's board of directors. Your wish is to put yourself out there and make the pitch. Perhaps you'll shine and become the "hero" who wins the new account. Whatever it is, write it down in three to four key words.

Now think about what it might be like to have everything work out. What would be the most positive outcome? You wind up apologizing to your husband's friend, who also takes responsibility for the dispute, gives you a hug, and asks that you both put it behind you. The conversation with your boss turns out to be much easier than expected; she thanks you for coming to talk to her and agrees to give you your highly deserved raise after all, and an additional bonus "just because." You make the presentation in front of the board of directors, prompting members of the board to give you a standing ovation and offer your firm the contract on the spot. Whatever your wish or concern, how would its realization make you feel? Would you feel proud? Satisfied? Joyful? Excited? Identify the best outcome and jot it down in a few key words. Now close your eyes and imagine the outcome as vividly as you can, writing down your thoughts as they occur to you. Give your images and thoughts free rein. Really let your mind go.

Of course, life doesn't always work out as we might like. So what prevents you from making your wish a reality? What is it in you that stands in the way? What is it in you that holds you back from fulfilling your wish? Is it the resentment you feel at knowing that your spouse keeps in touch with his college friends and you don't? Is it a fear you have about asserting yourself, especially when dealing with people in positions of power? Is it your tendency when speaking in public to recall all those times during your childhood when your older brother told you, "Nobody cares what you have to say"?

Think twice: Did you focus on your real obstacle? Is there another issue that feels even more critical? Dig as deep as you can and identify the critical hurdle in your path. Keep it in your mind's eye. Then imagine encountering this obstacle. Again give your fantasies free rein. Imagine the relevant events and scenarios as vividly as you can.

Keep in mind that there is no single, objectively valid, "correct" obstacle. You're simply looking for the obstacle in you that feels the most pertinent in the moment, and that gets you past any and all excuses you might make for yourself. When you hit on it, you'll know, because you'll experience a sense of insight or energized calmness, maybe even an epiphany.

Back in 1990, when my research was first beginning to show that positive fantasies were not helping people achieve their wishes, I was disappointed. I had embarked on studying dreams not merely because I found them interesting, but because I had hoped that dreaming might help people who were having trouble achieving wishes large and small. It was difficult to focus my work on fantasies knowing that they made individuals continue to struggle, so I wondered if there was anything I could do to the process of dreaming to turn things around and make dreams more helpful for achieving wishes. In particular, since positive fantasies tended to relax people, was there a way that I could use dreaming to wake them up, get them into gear, and motivate them to succeed?

I reasoned that the best way to get people up and moving was to ask them to dream and then to confront them right away with the realities that stood in the way of their dreams. I called this confrontation "mental contrasting." If I could ground fantasies in reality through mental contrasting, I might be able to circumvent the calming effects of dreaming and mobilize dreams as a tool for prompting directed action.

To see if there was anything to my idea, I needed to test mental contrasting in experimental studies. Yet I wasn't sure how. Psychologists often design studies by borrowing questionnaires, experimental procedures, and theoretical paradigms that other scholars have already developed and validated. When studying the relaxing effects of positive fantasies, for instance, I measured people's systolic blood pressure, since previous research had already established a relationship between systolic blood pressure and how emotionally "energized" a person was.[1] Mental contrasting was a new idea, so I had to devise my own ways of inducing and measuring it in people—what researchers call "operationalizing the variables." Although fun and an opportunity to be creative, this was also nerve-wracking. Conducting a study involved an outlay of time and money, and I had no idea what kind of outcome we'd get. If I didn't design the experiment correctly, I might not walk away with meaningful results.

I spent a good deal of time drawing models of experiments and researching possible paradigms for the studies. Since I wanted to discount alternative explanations, I would have to include a number of control groups. First, hypothesizing that the *combination* of dreaming and visualizing obstacles would prove helpful to people, not just the future fantasizing or the dwelling on reality alone, I decided to include a control group of people who only fantasized about the future and another of people who only thought about the reality. I also suspected that the realities in people's lives would take on meaning as obstacles only if people thought about them *after* they fantasized about wish fulfillment. Otherwise, the realities would feel neutral; people would not understand them as "standing in the way" of a happy ending. Only once they had mentally explored the happy ending, experiencing the relief and joy of attaining it, would they grasp something in their present life as an obstacle in the fullest sense. To test this idea, I created a third control group of people who "reverse contrasted" by starting imagining with the reality and then fantasizing. If mental contrasting worked, I'd see behavior change in individuals who mentally contrasted but not in individuals from the other groups.

A separate issue was how to elicit fantasies from participants in the studies. What should the fantasies be about, and what words should I use when asking participants to fantasize? I became obsessed with these questions for weeks, puzzling over them at odd moments throughout the day. I thought about the contents of my own fantasies and those of my students, and I queried people I knew about their wishes and concerns. Most of my friends and acquaintances told me about relationship, academic, or professional wishes: asking someone out on a date, getting along better with a relative or spouse, doing well on a test, starting or finishing an article. Realizing that different people were most passionate about very different kinds of wishes, I decided to start by not instructing people to dream about any particular desired future. If I let participants spontaneously generate their own wishes, the wishes they felt passionate about, they would wind up with the fullest, most developed fantasies.

I also realized that people felt obliged to reflect rationally on their emotions or feelings as they were having them. My friends and acquaintances were having trouble launching right away into dreams; their mental faculties constantly intruded, leading to doubts about which wish, outcome, and obstacle they should put down and how to best frame each of them. Often individuals switched midstream between different wishes or came up with a whole array of outcomes and obstacles, losing themselves in the question of which outcomes and obstacles were most important. In asking study participants to dream, I would need to frame the instructions carefully so that they experienced a free-flowing stream of images—what William James termed "the stream of thought, of consciousness, or of subjective life"[2]—without intruding thoughts or reflections about what they were or should be doing.

I decided to ask participants in some of the studies to come up with a few key words about the positive outcomes of their wishes and the obstacles that stood in the way. This procedure had an additional advantage: Some of my colleagues might have argued that the mere naming of a positive future and obstacle may be enough to cause energization and behavior change; I thought a couple of words weren't enough—the magic was in the mental elaboration of the desired outcome and the obstacle through free association (in other words, in the imagery generated). To see if I was right, I had all participants give us key words around their outcomes and obstacles, but only participants in the mental contrasting group would elaborate meditatively on the outcomes and obstacles. If the naming of future and reality was enough, and the elaboration through imagery wasn't vital, then all the groups should see the same effects, not just the mental contrasting group.

After weeks of preparation, my collaborators and I conducted a study with 168 female students at two Berlin universities.[3] After asking them to name their most important interpersonal wish or concern at the moment, we prompted the students to rate from 0 to 100 percent how likely they felt they were to achieve the wish. Each participant generated four sets of positive future key words she associated with fulfilling her wish (e.g., "having more time for each other," "feeling loved," or "feeling needed") and four negative reality key words associated with an obstacle to the wish (e.g., "being shy," "being too emotional," "having too much work"). One group of students was asked to mentally contrast by fantasizing about two positive future and two negative reality key words, alternating between the two (starting with a positive future key word), and writing down what came to mind. We specifically told these students: "Take as much time and space as you need to describe the scenario. If you need more space to write, please use the back of the page."

That was the mental contrasting group of research participants. A second group of students fantasized only about the four key words relating to the successful realization of each of their wishes (indulging), a third group fantasized only about the four key words relating to the reality that stood in the way (dwelling), and a fourth group "reverse contrasted" by first mentally elaborating on a negative reality key word and then a positive future key word, performing this process twice. Immediately afterward, all participants were asked to think about their interpersonal wishes or concerns and rate how energetic and active they felt. Two weeks after the experiment, we sent out a questionnaire asking participants to list all the actions they had taken since the experiment to bring their wishes to fruition. The participants indicated which two steps were hardest and when exactly they had performed these actions.

The results were surprising. We had expected that mental contrasting would give all participants who tried it a boost, but when we pored through the data, we saw that only *some* students who had mentally contrasted wound up feeling more energized and immediately tried to realize their wishes. The key was whether they thought they stood a good chance of success to begin with. If students had expectations based on past experience that they would succeed, then mental contrasting caused them to be significantly more energized and more promptly engaged than members of the other groups. If students who had mentally contrasted judged success unlikely, then they felt less energized and took less action around their wishes than did other participants (see fig. 2).

On the basis of this experiment, mental contrasting seemed even more helpful than we anticipated. If you think about it, you don't always want to be fired up to achieve a wish. If the wish is unlikely or even impossible to attain, isn't it better to let it go and focus on another wish that you can make headway with? If you're outstanding at basketball but not very skilled in music, and you'd like to find an activity where you can excel, does it make sense to spend four hours a day practicing violin

Interpersonal Concern

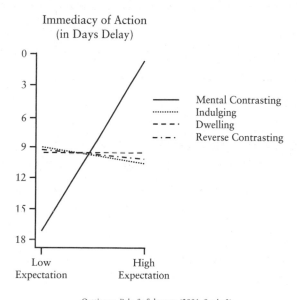

Immediacy of Action
(in Days Delay)

— Mental Contrasting
.... Indulging
– – – Dwelling
– · – · Reverse Contrasting

Low Expectation   High Expectation

Oettingen, Pak, & Schnetter (2001, Study 3).
Journal of Personality and Social Psychology, 80, 736–753.

Figure 2. The higher their expectations of success, the sooner mental contrasting participants tried to resolve their concern. No such relation emerged in participants of the control conditions (indulging, dwelling, and reverse contrasting).

in hopes of getting admitted to Juilliard? Think of the frustration you'd feel at being rejected by the admissions committee over and over again. Wouldn't it be better to aim at a wish you could achieve that also resonated with you, like becoming the starting center on your community college's basketball team?

It seems people benefit most from pursuing not just any wish, but a feasible wish. Certainly you know people who pursue dreams they stand little chance of achieving, subjecting themselves to years of disappointment before finally letting these dreams go and happily pursuing other, more attainable dreams. One friend of mine, Kevin, had a father who was the founder and CEO of a large corporation. When Kevin was ten years old, his father, in his early forties, passed away after a heart attack. Ever since then, Kevin dreamed of starting his own wildly successful company. Kevin had good grades in school and upon graduating had what he thought was an incredible idea for a new Web-based service. He tried to find banks that would loan him the money he needed to get the business off the ground, but all of them turned him down, claiming that his service was too similar to others already on the market. He turned to family and friends and was able to get some money, but not as much as he needed to promote his service properly. Several years went by, and although Kevin had been able to support himself, he had very little to show for his efforts. Finally he had enough. He got an MBA from a respectable school and snared an entry-level position at a large company. Today he isn't an entrepreneur or a CEO, but he has a well-paying job as a mid-level manager that he enjoys. He realizes that starting a company may have been his father's destiny, but it wasn't his. After a few bumps, he found his own path in life, and he couldn't be happier.

By the early 1990s, psychologists had researched the question of how to motivate people, but they had hardly looked at how to get people to disengage on a daily basis when the situation warranted it. Our study suggested that mental contrasting could help people do both things: engage even more forcefully when it made sense to engage, disengage even more clearly when that made sense. It functioned as a self-regulation tool, helping people allocate their energy more efficiently so they didn't merely pursue wishes, but *wisely* pursued them. People whose ideas for new businesses really were new and practicable would feel even more energized to put together business plans, seek investors, and move ahead with their start-up companies. Others, like Kevin, who sensed on some level that being an entrepreneur was not a good fit, would stand a better chance of finding the right wish, sparing themselves the years of fruitless and ultimately misguided effort.

Beyond long-term projects like starting your own business, I suspected that mental contrasting would help with many kinds of everyday difficulties. A person in a relationship that isn't quite working could do mental contrasting, grasp the obstacles in himself that prevent him from experiencing more harmony with his partner, and disengage, freeing himself to pursue another, more satisfying relationship. Or suppose a schoolteacher was waiting in line for coffee before her 8 a.m. class and there were ten people in front of her. She could either wait it out and be late or forgo the coffee and make it to her class on time. If she did mental contrasting, maybe she'd realize that she was okay being late for class. On the other hand, she might realize that she actually did want to be on time for class. In that case, she'd disengage from her wish of getting a coffee, resolving to get one after class instead. Whatever she wound up doing, she'd be doing it with full force. She'd find the path that was right for her and go for it. What if everybody used this tool? Wouldn't life be easier, richer, and more fulfilling each and every day? That's the potential I saw in mental contrasting.

Validating the Theory

Before I could promote mental contrasting to people as a self-regulatory tool to ease their daily life and enhance their long-term development, I needed to confirm that my initial results held up with different kinds of wishes and different ways of measuring engagement with a wish. First, I explored wishes in which people would find it especially easy to generate positive fantasies, testing what effect mental contrasting would have on how energized people felt to achieve a wish.

I began by going to a modeling agency, of all places, and asking them to give us photographs of attractive young male models. Assembling panels of female students, I asked them to rank these models based on how fascinating, handsome, and sympathetic they found them. A lucky young model who had *clearly* made our panels swoon received the highest total score.

I then recruited a different sample of 143 female first-year university students and showed them a picture of the attractive young man.[4] I accompanied his picture with some made-up information: he was "Michael S.," twenty-seven years old, and a doctoral candidate at the same institution where I was conducting this study, the Max Planck Institute for Human Development and Education in Berlin. Michael S. was undertaking a study of his own and actively seeking female participants. Any of the women in our study were free, if they wished, to meet Michael S. and be a part of his study, too. I included this last piece of information because I wanted participants to think that they might actually be able to meet Michael S.

Participants first looked at the picture of Michael S. for a couple of minutes and then proceeded to complete a three-part questionnaire. To measure their expectations about being able to get to know Michael S., I asked them questions like "If you came across this person, how likely do you think it is that you would get to know him on a personal level?" I also asked participants to rate how attractive, sympathetic, and interesting they found Michael S.

Then came the fun part: I invited participants to imagine that they had actually met Michael S. and had the opportunity to get to know him. They were asked to write down six key words conveying how wonderful they felt it would be to become acquainted with him (e.g., "the feeling of 'clicking' with someone") followed by six key words conveying obstacles that might prevent them from getting to know him (e.g., "my shyness," "I am not attractive enough to engage Michael's attention").

Similar to the previously described study, one group of participants had to go deeper and elaborate on two of the key words relating to the future (this time, getting to know Michael S.) and two key words relating to the obstacles they might face. They wrote down free thoughts and images, alternating between elaborating on positive future and negative reality key words. A second group only produced thoughts and images for four of the positive future key words (indulging). A third group only elaborated on the obstacles to meeting Michael S. (dwelling). And a fourth group—what I called the "no fantasy, no reality" group—did a series of absorbing arithmetic tasks. A week later, participants in all four groups filled out a questionnaire. To measure how energized and committed they were, I asked questions about how much the women wanted to get to know Michael S. and how disappointed they would be if they never got to meet him. The more participants felt they had a good chance of getting to know Michael S., the more eager they were to meet him. This result supported the established understanding in psychology that positive expectations about fulfilling a wish increase effort as well as the chances of achieving the wish. But those women with high expectations of success who had mentally contrasted (elaborating on both their fantasies of meeting Michael S. and the obstacles) saw a much greater spike in their eagerness than the other groups. They also saw a greater spike in their anticipated disappointment at not meeting him as their expectations increased. Mental contrasting *intensified* the effect that positive expectations about the future would ordinarily have. Just fantasizing or dwelling on the obstacles—or participating in an absorbing task that precluded any fantasizing or dwelling—failed to fire the women up to act. Likewise, women with low expectations of meeting Michael were less eager to meet him and anticipated less disappointment at not meeting him if they had mentally contrasted. They had disengaged from a wish that to them seemed unattainable (see fig. 3).

Getting to Know an Attractive Person

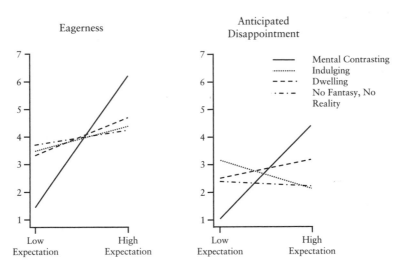

Oettingen (2000, Study 1). *Social Cognition, 18,* 101–129.

Figure 3. The higher their expectations of success, the more eager mental contrasting participants were to get to know Michael S. (left) and the more they anticipated disappointment in case of failure (right). No such relations were observed in the control conditions (indulging, dwelling, and no fantasy, no reality).

When we studied positive fantasies, we established their re-laxing effect on a physiological level by showing that systolic blood pressure actually declined after dreaming. A. Timur Se-vincer and I did a similar study for mental contrasting, taking blood pressure readings from sixty-three students in Germany before and after they completed a mental elaboration exercise.[5] In this case, we had two groups, a mental contrasting group and a group of students who only elaborated on their positive fanta-sies. Students who had only indulged in their fantasies tended to see declines in their blood pressure regardless of how likely they thought they were to accomplish their wishes; indulging in fanta-sies made them more relaxed. With students who had mentally contrasted, a different pattern of results held: the more attainable a goal seemed, the more blood pressure went up after the mental contrasting exercise. Mental contrasting provided students with resources on a physiological level if they were up to pursuing an achievable goal, while sparing the resources if their goal was un-achievable. Subsequent research established that the effects on blood pressure lasted for at least twenty minutes.[6]

To confirm whether people who mentally contrasted would perform objectively better than those who had either indulged or dwelled when wish fulfillment seemed likely, we invited ninety male students at German vocational schools for com-puter science to participate in a study of daydreams they had about math.[7] We asked students to rate how likely it was that they would get better in math, and also how much that outcome mattered to them. We had them list four positive outcomes of getting better in math; participants mentioned things like "more knowledge," "having a feeling of pride," and "being better qualified to get a job." We also had the students list four nega-tive aspects of reality that stood in their path to becoming math whizzes. They responded with items like "being lazy," "being absentminded," and "getting distracted by other students."

As before, we randomly split students into three groups and had these groups mentally contrast, indulge, or dwell based on the lists they had created. Two weeks later, we checked in with teachers for an assessment on how much individual students had buckled down in math and how much progress they had made. On a scale from 1 (not at all true) to 5 (very true), teachers rated how well the following statements applied to each student over the past two weeks: "The student was intrinsically interested in mathematics"; "The student showed persistent effort in studying mathematics"; "The student was easily distracted." We also asked teachers what grade they'd give each student if they had to fill out a report card that very day.

As we predicted, students who had mentally contrasted tried harder if they felt that success was likely, and they also achieved more in the opinion of their teachers. Those who had indulged in positive fantasies or dwelled on negative reality did not alter their effort as their expectations of success increased, nor did their actual performance change. Imagine how frustrating it must have been for those in the indulging group: in their dreams, they had mentally experienced themselves excelling and feeling relief as their math woes dissipated; then, as they took no action, they became stuck in their same old situation and did not fulfill their dreams in real life.

Other Beneficial Effects of Mental Contrasting

Our experiments were bearing out my ideas about mental contrasting, but I was curious about situations when people faced not external obstacles but rather obstacles or impediments related to their emotions or beliefs. For instance, many people feel reluctant to ask others for help, not because others wouldn't give them help but because for one reason or another they feel uncomfortable making the request.[8] One British study[9] has found that men don't seek assistance from pharmacists and primary care doctors as much as women do. Reporting on the research, the British newspaper *The Guardian* noted that "More men than women admit that their understanding of medicines is poor, and they are twice as likely to take a new prescription medicine without first reading the patient information leaflet or seeking professional advice." Ninety percent of men in the study "do not like to trouble a doctor or pharmacist unless they have a serious problem," and so don't take much advantage of preventative care.[10]

College students are another group of individuals who often don't seek out help for problems they may face.[11] The same is true for children and adolescents. According to a publication by the National Association of School Psychologists, ". . . a wealth of findings highlights the limited use of mental health services by adolescents with emotional and behavioral problems."[12] Other research has revealed that schoolchildren don't always seek out the help they need in the classroom, and their learning suffers as a result.[13]

Online blogs and bulletin boards reveal the tremendous anguish and turmoil that surrounds the simple act of asking for assistance from colleagues, peers, or even loved ones. As one overwhelmed mother remarks: "I don't understand why I don't ask for more help or make more 'me' time. . . . What is my problem? I have been with my husband for eight years and married for almost five, and he has always been there the very few times I asked for help (I can think of maybe three to four times).

I feel like I should spearhead the creation of a support group for working mothers who do not ask for help."[14] Another woman confides that "For as long as I can remember I've run away from all forms of assistance. From the 'Let me do it!' response I would have as a child whenever my parents tried to help me with a task I was struggling with, to trying on tiptoe to reach the cereal on the top shelf at the grocery store rather than asking the clerk to get it down, to pretending I understand something only to spend hours later trying to figure it out on my own."[15]

We asked 135 undergraduate students to name a school-related challenge they wanted to address within the next couple of weeks ("passing a tough exam" and "getting an internship" were typical responses).[16] Then they had to identify an individual who could help them with the task—referred to as "Person X" during the rest of the experiment. To measure participants' expectations, we asked them to numerically rate how likely Person X would be to help them. As in our other mental contrasting studies, we had participants list positive future outcomes that would accrue if they successfully asked for help, as well as aspects of "present reality" that impeded them from asking for help. We randomly assigned students to do one of three mental exercises based on elements from these lists: mentally contrast, indulge exclusively in their fantasies, or dwell solely on the realities that impeded them from asking for help. We instructed all participants to imagine their outcomes and/or obstacles as completely as possible, unleashing free thoughts and images, and taking as much time and space as they needed to write down what occurred to them.

Two weeks later, we sent out follow-up questionnaires, which two-thirds of participants sent back to us. We asked them to rate how much headway they made on their challenges with the assistance of Person X. As compared with students who indulged and dwelled, those who had mentally contrasted reported attaining much more help if they also thought that they were likely to receive it. Mental contrasting enabled students with strong expectations of receiving help to ask for and obtain the assistance they required. Students who didn't expect to get help asked for less of it—which saved them needless effort and frustration.

So far, I have discussed research demonstrating that mental contrasting can work with existing expectations that people have accumulated over their lives to help them decide between different options and to move toward their desired futures. Think about the full implications of this phenomenon. So often in life, people become influenced by their past experiences; what has already happened to them places limitations on what they feel they can achieve. Often, these limitations are helpful, but sometimes they're not, impeding us from moving toward wishes whose fulfillment might improve our lives and are in fact attainable.

Think about a man who had a couple of bad experiences playing tennis as a boy. He might forgo opportunities to play tennis as adult, even though with a couple of lessons he could have a great time and develop a new hobby. Even more significantly, a person who had always been told he wasn't as smart as other people might not bother to graduate from college, thinking that it wouldn't help him anyway in his career, since there were certain jobs he just couldn't hope to do well in. How tragic is it that he settles for a low-paying job because he can't overcome his ingrained expectations?

Sometimes expectations are so ingrained that they are very difficult to dislodge. People tend to think, based on past experience, that they aren't likely to succeed at a specific wish, and they wind up feeling depressed and disengaged in general. What if in these situations we could get people energized around a different wish where it is unclear what their chances of success are? We might not be able to help the individual graduate from college if he has always been told he won't make the cut, but perhaps we could get him excited about a field or activity that he doesn't have much experience with. We could at least provide him with an initial positive experience that would then over time lead him to engage more and possibly allow him to discover a new passion.

My son Anton had never thought much about singing. One day in church, he spontaneously sang along with the congregation. A woman sitting next to him said, "You have an impressive voice. You should get singing lessons." She connected Anton to a teacher, and ever since, Anton has taken lessons. He now has a passion for singing that might never have taken root had he not had that initial positive experience that set up expectations of future success.

In effect, the woman sitting next to Anton awakened his expectations by providing him with positive feedback. People often use feedback in this way as a tool to prop up expectations. In the workplace, managers turn to positive feedback to instill self-confidence in their subordinates when they are stretching to achieve new goals. Coaches spur their charges to reach beyond where they are presently by telling them, "You can do it!" Decades of research in psychology have established how potent positive feedback is as a means of enhancing expectations.[17] I wondered whether mental contrasting could help translate positive feedback into actual performance even better than positive feedback alone.

I turned to an area that seems to have occasioned heightened public concern in recent years: the apparent decline in creativity among American schoolchildren. The economic consequences of such a decline seem high; corporate executives have affirmed in surveys that creativity and innovation are key skills they wish to build in their workforces.[18] In a twenty-first-century knowledge economy, will our country remain competitive economically without millions of bright, engaged, and creative individuals showing up for work each day? That doesn't even begin to account for the personal satisfaction of creativity and the cultural contributions that creative people make. Some commentators have even seen creativity as a source of healthfulness and longevity.[19]

I chose to study creativity for another reason: many people don't have strong expectations about whether or not they are creative. A few people are told as youngsters that they are especially creative, but schools often don't make a point of testing for creativity as they do for general intelligence or academic ability. Many Americans know how they did on standardized tests such as the SAT or ACT, but they have only a vague sense of how likely they are to come up with entirely new and different solutions to a problem that confronts them or how likely they are to generate new connections between unrelated terms or concepts. Let's say you're an accountant. Would you necessarily have any idea about your ability to create from scratch a new appetizer dish for the dinner you are hosting? Would you feel confident in your ability to paint a picture or write a poem? Most people probably wouldn't. Creativity would seem to be precisely an area where it might be possible to bolster expectations, and thus move people forward toward goals.

My collaborators and I invited 158 college students to take

part in a study involving various tasks and exercises; participants were working in separate computer cubicles.[20] We flashed words on-screen from a popular questionnaire used by psychologists to measure creativity called the Creative Personality Scale (CPS),[21] and had students rate the extent to which these words applied to them (examples: "inventive," "insightful"). After collecting the students' responses to these words, we gave one group of randomly chosen participants very positive feedback about their creative talents. "Out of a possible score of 31 points, you have received 28 points," we told them. "You are in the ninetieth percentile of the population. Your creative potential is far better than average." A second group received only moderately positive feedback; we told them that they received 15 points on our creativity test, which put them in the sixtieth percentile of the population, only "a little better than average."

We proceeded much as we had in the previous mental contrasting studies. We measured students' expectations about their success on the creativity tasks we were going to give them, asking them to rate both how likely they were to succeed on the tasks, and how much their success on the tasks mattered to them. Then we induced mental contrasting, indulging, or dwelling in the usual fashion and encouraged participants to freely associate in the respective ways.

Finally, we tested students' creative performance by giving them twenty-four problems to solve, three sets of eight problems each. First, students tackled verbal problems, then mathematical problems, and then spatial problems, with ten minutes for each category. We utilized problems from an earlier test we'd given that had revealed that these problems were modestly difficult and required at most three minutes to solve. As an example, one mathematical problem read "Describe how to put 27 animals in 4 pens in such a way that there will be an odd number of animals in each pen."[22]

Since we had measured students' actual creative potential using the CPS scale, we were able to statistically adjust for that variable. We found that mental contrasting did indeed enhance the impact of positive feedback. Mental contrasting students who had been told they were extremely creative solved significantly more problems in the allotted time than those who indulged or dwelled—6.5 problems as opposed to about 5 problems in the case of participants who had indulged, and about 4 problems in the case of participants who had dwelled. Participants who had received the positive feedback and did the mental contrasting exercise also solved more problems than any of the students in the group that had received marginally positive feedback.

The results of this study struck me as compelling, but in fact we had neglected one possibility: What if positive feedback alone was enough to boost creative performance, without the help of mental contrasting? To test for this alternative explanation of our results, we would need to include a group of students who hadn't performed any of our fantasy realization strategies. We undertook a second experiment that was identical except that we had a fourth group of students perform a dummy exercise; students alternated between mentally elaborating on positive and negative attributes of a landscape picture. The pattern of results in this study was the same: students who mentally contrasted and who had received positive feedback solved more creativity problems than students in any of the other groups. Mental contrasting made all the difference, not the positive feedback in and of itself.

Negative Future Fantasies

The studies I've discussed thus far assume that people readily generate positive fantasies. I think that's probably true, although there are times when some or perhaps all of us have difficulty dreaming. Many of us go through periods when we're depressed or anxious, and it seems like nothing can ever change for the good. Even people who aren't depressed or anxious might have areas in their lives where it never occurs to them to dream of a positive future because they are used to thinking only negatively—areas in life where at an extreme they feel as if nothing will ever change and there is no hope for the future. In such areas, we tend to generate negative, anxious fantasies of making mistakes, suffering, and feeling trapped.

A shy man in his forties, for instance, might despair of never being outgoing enough in social situations to strike up a relationship with a woman and eventually get married. A police officer seriously injured in the line of duty and forced to retire might write off the idea that he will ever find a career he loves as much as being a policeman. A student who can't seem to do well on a math test will freeze up in exam situations, overcome by anxiety and negative fantasies of doing poorly yet again. A small child might fear going to the pediatrician because she dreads the vaccine she knows will be administered.

Ever since I had visited East Germany, I had been interested in situations where people had given in to their fears and had a hard time generating positive fantasies. I wondered: Could mental contrasting help people whose wish was not to reach a positive state but rather to confront a negative future straight on, so that their unjustified fears would go away?

We often see people harboring unjustified fears of individuals from social or ethnic groups that are different from theirs. All over the world, these fears cause members of different groups to avoid one another, even to hate or fight with one another. In Germany and other European countries, xenophobia is a serious problem, leading to street fights between youths and the rise of groups with violent ideologies.[23] We asked 158 youths in an ethnically homogenous part of Berlin to participate in a study.[24] We first had them read the following text:

> There are a lot of foreign people living in Berlin, such as immigrants, persons seeking political asylum, or civil war refugees. The number of foreigners residing within the several districts varies, with Weißensee as the district where the smallest number of foreigners reside. Therefore, in the future, immigrants and people seeking asylum may primarily be placed in Weißensee, and several hostels for refugees may be established in Weißensee within the next year. This study will find out if the citizens of Weißensee are willing to accept foreigners in their district. We are especially interested in adolescents' thoughts and beliefs.

To test how likely participants thought it was that they would overcome fears about foreigners, we asked them point-blank: "If several hostels for refugees were established in Weißensee within the next year, how likely do you think it is that you would help to integrate the foreigners in Weißensee?"

Next, participants generated negative fantasies in response to the following:

> Please imagine that in Weißensee several hostels for immigrants and people seeking political asylum have just been established. Now think about what negative consequences this would have for you personally. How might things for you change for the worse? What repercussions might you suffer from? How might this interfere with your everyday life? Please give your images, fantasies, and thoughts free rein. Then describe these negative thoughts and images about the future in writing on the following page. If you need more space, please continue on the back of the paper.

To help students generate images of the positive reality that stood in the way of the negative dreams coming true, we showed them twelve statements that appeared to come from adolescents who had already experienced foreigners moving into their neighborhoods. These statements described positive relations between the adolescents and foreigners (e.g., "Playing soccer with these guys was just great. Finally, we had strong and fair opponents," or "When arriving at the new apartment with our furniture, two foreigners volunteered to help us to carry the heavy stuff upstairs").

At this point, we had one group of students perform mental contrasting, while another indulged in their fearful fantasies about immigrants moving in, and a third mentally elaborated only on the positive realities that stood in the way of the fearful fantasies becoming real. Students who were to fixate on the negative future were given a statement intended to disparage the positive reality: "What problem does the interviewed person want to conceal? Please describe your thoughts!" We prompted students who were to dwell on the positive reality to take the adolescents' statements especially seriously by giving them the following instruction: "Please describe your thoughts that speak for the notion that you would get along with the foreigners in Weißensee."

Two weeks after this exercise, we contacted all participants and measured their level of tolerance for foreigners by asking, "If several hostels for refugees were established in Weißensee within the next year, how harmful would it be to you?" We also measured how willing participants would be to exert the effort to get to know foreigners, asking them how interested they would be in reading a journal created collaboratively with the foreign adolescents, and how many hours a week they'd be willing to spend writing and editing the journal themselves. Finally, we measured how many plans students made to interact with foreigners despite their fears by analyzing their responses to the following question: "Please think about what it would be like to live with the foreign adolescents in your district. Give your thoughts and images free rein, and describe all these thoughts and images. If you need more space to write, please use the back page."

As we expected, students in the mental contrasting group who judged it likely that they would be able to overcome their fears about foreigners were more tolerant, were more willing to exert effort, and made more plans to engage with the foreign adolescents, while those with lower initial expectations who had mentally contrasted did not differ from the control groups (see fig. 4).

Improving Tolerance

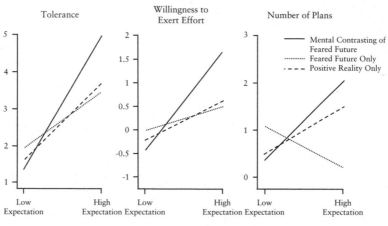

Oettingen, Mayer, Thorpe, Janetzke, & Lorenz (2005, Study 2).
Motivation and Emotion, 29, 237–267.

Figure 4. The higher their expectations of success, the more participants who mentally contrasted their feared future showed tolerance (left), willingness to exert effort (middle), and formed plans (right) to welcome their foreign peers. No such relations emerged in participants of the control conditions (indulging in the feared future only and dwelling on the positive reality only).

Just a few minutes of mental contrasting helped students overcome an anxious and unjustified fantasy and approach the object of their fears. Given how pervasive xenophobia is, not to mention how many individuals suffer from an endless variety of other unjustified or overblown fears, it's exciting to think that mental contrasting might provide an easy, cheap, and effective way of confronting those fears head on and engaging more fully with life.

Try this exercise for yourself. Think about a fear you have about the future that is vexing you quite a bit and that you know is unjustified. Summarize your fear in three to four words. For instance, suppose you're a father who has gotten divorced and you share custody with your ex-wife, who has gotten remarried. For the sake of your daughter's happiness, you want to become friendly with her stepfather, but you find yourself stymied by your own emotions. Your fear might be "My daughter will become less attached to me and more attached to her stepfather." Now go on to imagine the worst possible outcome. In this case, it might be "I feel distanced from my daughter. When I see her she ignores me, but she eagerly spends time with her stepfather." Okay, now think of the positive reality that stands in the way of this fear coming true. What in your actual life suggests that your fear won't really come to pass? What's the single key element? In this case, it might be "The fact that my daughter is extremely attached to me and loves me, and it's obvious to anyone around us." Close your eyes and elaborate on this reality.

Now take a step back. Did the exercise help? I think you'll find that by being reminded of the positive reality standing in the way, you will be less transfixed by the anxious fantasy. When I conducted this kind of mental contrasting with people in Germany, they reported that the experience was soothing, akin to taking a warm bath or getting a massage. "It just made me feel so much calmer and more secure," one woman told me. "I sense that I am more grounded and focused."

Mental contrasting can produce results with both unjustified fears as well as overblown fears rooted in a kernel of truth. If as a child you suffered through a couple of painful visits to the dentist, you might today fear going to get a filling replaced, and this fear might become so terrorizing that you put off taking care of your dental needs until you just cannot avoid it. Mental contrasting will help you in this case to approach the task of going to the dentist. But if your fear is justified, then mental contrasting will confirm this, since there is nothing preventing your fear from coming true. The exercise will then help you to take preventive measures or avoid the impending danger altogether.

One caveat: mental contrasting is most appropriate for unjustified fears that are strong and debilitating. A great deal of research has shown that a total lack of anxiety detracts from performance, just as extreme anxiety does (especially when the task in question is complex).[25] If you're a student who experiences debilitating anxiety around taking tests, mental contrasting can help you approach the object of your fears so that you can perform better. But if you experience only mild to moderate anxiety, you may benefit from feeling a bit of anxiety, and mentally contrasting your fears may leave you feeling too relaxed and not sufficiently motivated to prepare. When trying mental contrasting to approach your own fears, I advise that you first make sure to honestly evaluate whether your fears are unjustified, or whether they might not spur you on to more effort and better performance.

Charlie's Story

A series of studies has revealed mental contrasting to be an effective strategy for fulfilling wishes—certainly far more effective than merely indulging in dreams about a happy future. I've shown this for a range of different wishes and contexts, from solving personal problems to vocational training to creativity. The research I've mentioned and other experiments I've conducted have upheld these findings for participants of different ages, socioeconomic status, and cultures, showing that mental contrasting brings insight into our real wishes and then increases energy and planning for actually achieving our dearest wishes and dreams.

What makes these results especially compelling is the nature of mental contrasting itself. Many people think that if you have difficulties realizing your wishes and achieving your goals, you need to spend months or years in therapy or do session after session with a coach or read endless self-improvement books. While these techniques may help, we achieved measurable results in our studies using an exercise that took between five and twenty minutes to complete (in everyday life, it will usually take even less time, as we shall see). Imagine what might happen if you got in the habit of performing quick mental contrasting exercises daily for all sorts of wishes, concerns, and anxieties, ranging from how you'd like to spend your evening to how you'd like to spend the next twenty years of your life.

Charlie, a graduate student, found mental contrasting especially helpful during a difficult period in which his grandmother was suffering from ovarian cancer. He moved back home to take care of her through two surgeries and an extended period of convalescence. During this time, he bore the burden of seeing to his grandmother's daily care, including attending to her IV and feeding tubes. "We got no sleep," he reported. "It was simply one of the most terrifying periods of my life—to see someone you care about like that. And it's not like you could talk to anyone about your feelings. Everyone in the family is trying to escape what is happening, and you don't want to burden your friends. More than anything else, I just wanted to cope with the experience so that I could be strong for my grandmother, but I didn't know how."

Charlie tried to deal with the stress by going to mental health professionals, but in his case, that didn't help much. "I was just looking for a friend to talk to about all the strange observations I had, but they were more interested in ancillary and seemingly meaningless issues, like how I felt about my parents. They were focused on the past, when all I wanted was to move forward. We just couldn't address things that I wanted to address." Charlie found comfort in mental contrasting, particularly its ability to confront him with the insecurities and other internal issues that were preventing him from coping. "It was like ripping the Band-Aid off right away, having to confront something that you spend a lot of time trying to keep at bay."

"I was having a hard time, for instance, taking time out for me, to keep myself healthy. I felt guilty asking my uncle to look after my grandmother for a few minutes so I could get away. Mental contrasting helped me come face-to-face with the real obstacle to that goal of getting away, which was the guilt I felt at simply *wanting* to get away. That was very helpful. It allowed me to recompose myself and give myself what I needed. I couldn't do anything about my grandmother's illness—she was going to die. But I could find ways of coping, so that I could handle her illness gracefully."

As Charlie expressed so convincingly, the path to realizing your wishes—however big or small they might be, whether they're felt in good times or in bad—is not to push your obstacles aside and focus only on your wishes, but rather to acknowledge *both* and bring them into contact with each other: first the wish, then the reality. When you do that, something wonderful happens. Working on your own, without the aid of a therapist, coach, or medications, you are energized to pursue wishes that you judge yourself capable of achieving (such as spending a few minutes away from a sick relative), and you face the reality of unattainable wishes (such as miraculously healing that relative). In the latter case, you free yourself to pursue more feasible wishes. You regulate your own path, engaging more fully in life, leading yourself over time to the wise pursuit of your dreams.

Chapter Five

. . . .

Engaging Our Nonconscious Minds

Dedicating yourself to a goal, disciplining yourself to take action, and making meaningful progress is supposed to be hard. Companies spend millions on executive coaching to help leaders overcome bad habits and interpersonal problems with little systematic research showing that coaching works.[1] Patients who want to stop smoking, lose weight, or overcome a gambling addiction can spend a decade trying any number of approaches and still fail. Can it really be that a mundane activity—taking a straightforward series of steps to "spoil" positive fantasies—yields significant changes in commitment to wishes, energy levels, and achievement? Can a few minutes spent imagining a wish big or small, long term or short term, and then the obstacle to attaining that wish really lead you to make wiser decisions and take more sensible, prudent actions? How can something so simple and easy make such a difference?

For scholars in psychology, the problem was not that mental contrasting was too simple, but that it was too complicated. Our findings upended the conventional wisdom that believing you are likely to succeed makes you more likely to move toward fulfilling a wish; as we showed, that link only holds true when people performed mental contrasting, not when they indulged in positive fantasies or dwelled on the negative reality. Many psychologists were used to thinking about motivation in a straightforward way: If you had more positive thinking, you got more motivation, action, and achievement. If you had less positive thinking, you got less motivation, action, and achievement. My research was painting a more nuanced picture, bringing together positive thoughts and images about the future with imaginings of a negative present reality.

Given how unfamiliar mental contrasting was and the pushback from my peers, I wanted to understand *how and why* it worked. Beyond that, the phenomenon of mental contrasting seemed striking enough to require exploration of the underlying mechanisms. Study participants repeatedly voiced how much they benefited from mental contrasting. We noticed how engaged they were while performing it and could see in their writings how deeply immersed they became in their imaginations. When, as part of a study, participants had to check back a couple of weeks later, often 80 percent to 90 percent of them would comply—a rate much higher than the norm for these types of experiments. Some student participants were so taken by mental contrasting that they went on to work as research assistants in my lab and attend graduate school in psychology.

Watching participants perform mental contrasting, we could tell by their facial expressions that something was happening in their minds. Often participants seemed to experience insights, their eyes brightening and their bodies straightening in their chairs, suggesting an unusual combination of relief and focus. I suspected that mental contrasting wasn't just working on a conscious level; it was engaging people's *nonconscious minds*, reshaping the very way they viewed reality. These nonconscious shifts in perception were making behavior changes possible for people in situations when they felt a wish was reachable—doing the work seemingly by magic, so that pursuing wishes was easy.[2] But what were these shifts in perception? What was happening on a cognitive level?

When Milliseconds Count

Think about an American couple in their late twenties, Nick and Liz. Nick is living in Brussels working as an international law specialist for the European Union, while Liz is in Boston pursuing her doctorate in education. Nick and Liz are serious about each other, and when they meet up for the holidays or a week's vacation in one or the other's city, they spend hours lying in bed or sitting in a café imagining a future life together— two kids, a nice colonial home in Vermont with red shutters, a high school principal's job for Liz and a college professorship for Nick, perhaps an apple orchard on their property, or at least enough space so that Nick can pursue his long-lost hobby of gardening. At other times, when they are not together, Nick and Liz focus less on these dreams and more on the real-life difficulties of pursuing a long-distance relationship. During their Skype conversations every day or so, they complain about feeling lonely and not being able to share the simple pleasures of life, such as an evening meal cooked at home. Nick misses cuddling with Liz and watching TV; Liz misses relaxing with Nick as well, and she longs for his company when she goes out at night. Sometimes they feel out of synch with each other, that their communication isn't working, and that their relationship is at risk of stagnating.

Nick and Liz continue on like this, alternating between periods of dreaming and frustration. And then one day, Nick has an epiphany. He realizes that his anxiety about leaving a good job is causing them to live thousands of miles away from each other. In effect, his anxiety is the primary obstacle that prevents them from attaining the bliss they envision. Nick mentions this to Liz during one of their Skype sessions, and she, too, shares in the epiphany. Now the two of them have a very different kind of conversation. It's clear that they can't continue living as they have been if they are to fulfill their dreams. They take stock of their situations and come to an agreement. Nick, who has risen as far as he can within the European Union anyway, will quit his job and apply for teaching positions in New England. Liz will speed up her work on her doctorate. They will get married the following year and begin saving for that white colonial while trying to start a family.

Take a peek at wedding announcements in the newspaper, and you will find stories like Nick and Liz's—couples in long-distance relationships who get married only after one partner makes the connection between the future wish of a shared life and the emotions underlying their separation. I initially speculated that the "magic" of mental contrasting lies in its ability to connect the future and reality without people becoming aware of it. By first imagining future wishes and then the present reality, we lead ourselves to consider whether we really can overcome the present conditions that obstruct our wishes, activating our expectations about the future based on past experience. When we think our wishes are feasible, the future and present reality become fused together on a nonconscious level; when they're not feasible, the future and present reality don't become fused but actually become disconnected.

Note that order plays a role here. I thought that reverse contrasting—thinking about the reality first and then the dream or wish—wouldn't create the association in a person's mind that "you need to overcome this obstacle to achieve that wish." A student who was thinking about receiving an invitation to a huge party, and who afterward thought about how nice it would be to pass her Philosophy 101 exam, might wonder about what kind of beer the host would have on tap. She wouldn't necessarily perceive the reality of the party (which would take time away from studying) as standing in the way of the wish of passing the exam. Reality and future would not be linked in her mind. And she wouldn't be especially inclined to pass up the party in order to study. But if she first thought of the wish of passing the exam, the invitation to the party *would* take on a whole new meaning. A nonconscious linkage between the wish and the obstacle would take hold.

With such a mental linkage in place, an individual couldn't think about her dream any longer without automatic reference to the obstacle, and the obstacle would serve as a constant and nonconscious spur to take action. Every time she thought of the wish, the wish would nonconsciously activate the reality, bringing resources to bear to move closer toward attaining the wish. In this way, mental contrasting would work beneath the rim of our consciousness to help us achieve tangible results in our lives. When the link between future and reality didn't get forged in a person's mind, or was only weakly forged, thinking about the wish wouldn't immediately activate notions of the reality standing in the way, so people would fail to do what is required to move closer to their wish.

My collaborator Andreas Kappes and I asked 134 college students to think about the most important wish they had for their social lives.[3] They mentioned things like "finding a girl-friend," "forming a close friendship with other students," "be-coming more independent." As in other studies, we asked students at the outset to rate how likely they thought they were to achieve these wishes. Then students listed words or phrases they associated with the best outcome (e.g., "joy and happi-ness," "trusting relationships") and words or phrases they asso-ciated with the reality standing in the way (e.g., "being shy," "having no time for myself"). Students reduced these phrases down to two individual words that summarized, respectively, the best outcome and their present reality (e.g., "happy" and "shy").

We asked some of the students to perform mental contrast-ing based on the best outcome and the reality they had iden-tified. A second group did reverse contrasting, imagining their present reality first and then their best outcome. A third group performed an irrelevant dummy exercise, first imagining a nice experience they had with a teacher at school and then an un-pleasant encounter with a teacher.

The next part of our experiment measured how strong the associations between future and reality were in participants' minds. We used what is called a "primed lexical decision task,"[4] which is to say we measured how quickly students, confronted with a string of letters—what we called the "target"—would identify whether it was a word or merely gibberish. The string of letters included, among others, the words that students had identified as summarizing their best outcome and reality. We placed a white cross on a black computer screen for 500 milliseconds and then presented a priming word (e.g., "happy," or "respect") for 50 milliseconds. At these speeds, participants perceived the priming word as a flash too quick to read. To further prevent their conscious minds from processing the priming word, we masked it by following the priming word with a random string of letters (e.g., ITGPBLF). Then, for a matter of milliseconds, we showed them the target in red. Participants had to make a "lexical decision," determining as quickly as they could whether the target flashed on the screen was a word or nonword. They did that by pressing one of two labeled keys in front of them (see fig. 5).

Primed Lexical Decision Task

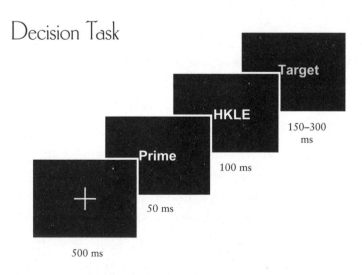

Figure 5. Course of events of a single trial in the primed lexical decision task.

As part of this exercise, we performed trials in which we first showed the priming word reflecting the participant's future wish and then the target reflecting her present reality. This would allow us to measure how strongly the participant's mind associated the future and the reality; if the link was strong, the participant would register the second, "reality" word much more quickly after having first been shown a brief flash of the "future" word. We also inserted various control trials as well as trials with nonwords as targets. In certain of the control trials, we reversed the order of words, seeking to measure how quickly flashing the "reality" word prompted responses to the "future" word.[5]

We concluded the experiment by measuring how strongly participants were pursuing their wishes. Participants answered questions about how energized or active they felt about realizing the wishes they had identified, how "in control" they felt of their wishes, and how certain they were about what they needed to do to realize their wishes.

The results of this experiment suggested that mental contrasting does indeed cause the present reality to be joined with successful wish fulfillment in people's minds. When students judged their future wishes to be feasible, they were quickest to react to the "reality" word they had been shown after first having been shown the "future" word. The reality was right there for them, imperceptibly linked to the positive fantasy that the "future" word was evoking. When students thought their wishes unfeasible, they were less quick to react. In fact, they were slower to react than students who had performed reverse contrasting and the dummy task. Mental contrasting weakened the connection between future and reality in their nonconscious minds.

It's worth noting that students with feasible wishes did not call up the "future" word any more quickly when first shown the "reality" word. Mental contrasting forged a link between the future and the reality, but it was specifically in this order: *first* future and *then* reality. Mental contrasting almost instantaneously brings the reality to mind when the future is called up—a process that is beyond our conscious ability to notice and control.

As we expected, students who had performed mental contrasting were more energized than other students when their wishes were feasible, and less energized when those wishes were far-fetched. The same was true for how "in control" and how clear participants felt about their wishes. The strength of the cognitive associations between future and reality in turn predicted how intensely students felt about pursuing their goals. Students who hadn't performed mental contrasting linked the future and reality in their minds to only a moderate extent and were only lukewarm about pursuing their wishes. This was true whether or not they thought their wishes were attainable.

What happens in those happy instances when people manage to actually achieve their wishes? Do the cognitive links between dream and present obstacle remain intact once they have already done their job? It would make sense for them to dissolve, since they are no longer needed as a source of energy or motivation.

To test this hypothesis, we probed the strength of cognitive associations in research participants who had mentally contrasted a specific wish and then had fulfilled that wish. We compared these participants with others who had performed mental contrasting but hadn't fulfilled their wishes. Recognizing that people almost universally want to think of themselves as creative, we asked 142 college students to read about what creativity is and how important it is for a person's future accomplishments. Telling them that we were giving them a creativity test, we asked them to rate how likely they would be to score higher than average. We had some students mentally contrast about their wish of scoring well on the test, elaborating on how great it would feel to learn that they were creative as well as on the realities that stood in the way (e.g., "fatigue" or "closed-mindedness"), while those in the control group imagined a positive and negative experience with one of their teachers. To influence students' beliefs about their own creativity, we gave them four creativity exercises to do, letting them know that over the past couple of years, over a thousand students at their university had completed the same test. Two minutes after they completed the exercises, they received their scores. Some of the students were informed that they were only in the forty-third percentile of scores—in other words, they had not achieved their wish of learning they were creative. Others were informed that they were in the eighty-seventh percentile and in fact were quite creative.

Afterward, we measured the cognitive associations between future and present reality using a primed lexical decision task similar to the one described earlier. Sure enough, the reaction times to the "reality" word after being primed with the "future" word was lower (indicating a *stronger* cognitive association between future and reality) for students who had performed mental contrasting and who expected to do well on the test than for respective students in the control group. But this finding only held true with students who had received poor results on their tests and thus had not attained their wishes. In students who had attained their wish of scoring highly on the test, there were no such differences in reaction times between the mental contrasting group and the control group (see fig. 6). This finding indicates that the cognitive association between future and reality had dissolved in the mental contrasting students. When we succeed at an endeavor, obstacles and wishes tend to become uncoupled in our minds. We move on, the wish receding from the forefront of our minds. The way becomes clear for other cognitive associations to form as we think about and pursue other wishes.

Future-Reality Association Proving Creative

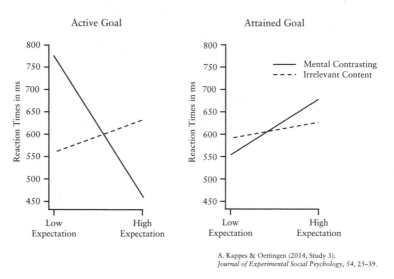

A. Kappes & Oettingen (2014, Study 3).
Journal of Experimental Social Psychology, 54, 25–39.

Figure 6. The higher their expectations of success, the stronger the cognitive associations between future and reality in participants who mentally contrasted, but not in those of the control group who fantasized about irrelevant content (left). This pattern of results faded when students had attained their goal (right).

I invite you to try a little experiment of your own. Think of a wish you have for the next week, one that you feel pretty confident you can achieve, but that you still find challenging. Perform mental contrasting, allowing yourself time to first identify the wish, identify and clearly imagine the best outcome, and then identify and imagine the present reality inside you that holds you back from achieving the wish. This might be a fear or anxiety, a sense of laziness, or perhaps an irritating habit. Slow down when imagining the outcome and present reality. Really let the images flow. Allow a day or two to pass, and try thinking again of having fulfilled your wish. Are you able to do so without the same obstacle coming to mind? At odd moments during the day when you think of the wished-for future, do you also think of the reality at more or less the same time? Does the reality jump out at you? Not everyone will notice that his or her dream has been "ruined" in this way; remember, this cognitive process is happening on a nonconscious level. But if you do notice yourself returning to the obstacle again and again, you can also feel assured that this is mental contrasting working on your behalf to help push you toward realizing your wish.

Taking the Stairs

Let's return to the story of the student who has a Philosophy 101 exam coming up but also an invitation to a blowout party. It's Saturday, and the exam is scheduled for the following Monday. Sitting in a library carrel, the student—let's call her Joni—daydreams about the exam, how amazing it would be to receive an A, how validated she would feel next to her roommate

Kathy, who always receives A's on exams and never seeks to remind others of that fact. Joni comes from a rural town in Indiana and is one of the few in her community to go to college. Getting an A on the exam would lock up an A for the entire course, which would in turn guarantee Joni a full scholarship for her second year. She could return home after her first semester in college to find her entire extended family—grandparents, aunts, uncles, cousins—taking pride in what she managed to accomplish at the top-flight college she attends. How wonderful it would be to tell her family about her successes, to see the pride and admiration in their eyes, and to repay them in a fashion for the support they have shown her. Also, if Joni receives an A in philosophy, she won't have to worry about maintaining the grade point average she needs to remain qualified for the scholarship she is receiving. She would feel so much more comfortable and secure returning to school for another semester.

Joni is good at philosophy—she did a term paper on John Stuart Mill as a high school senior—so she's pretty sure that studying hard and well will allow her to score the A. But then she thinks of the party scheduled for that night. All her friends are going, and all intend to get trashed. It's the end of the semester, and most of her friends have finished their exams. The host plans to have a popular local band play a three-hour show as part of the party. There will be hundreds of people there, including all the cutest boys from Joni's dorm. But if she goes to that party, she knows she will be so hungover that Sunday will be lost entirely as study time, and she might not feel that great on exam day, either. She still has reams of material to cover on the enlightenment and romantic philosophers. There's no way she can do that before the party. Rousseau alone will take three or four hours.

The answer, unpleasant as it is, is clear: she must skip the party, or at the very least arrive late and drink only ginger ale. Okay, skipping is a bit draconian. She'll arrive late, put a beer in her hand, and sip until midnight, when she'll make an early exit. She's done this before, her friends didn't care that much, and she received strong grades on previous tests. Perfect. Sipping from a beer all night is the "instrumental behavior" Joni needs to achieve her wish.

Forging a link between the desired future and present reality isn't the only way mental contrasting acts on our nonconscious minds. Our research has also established that mental contrasting forges powerful, nonconscious associations between the obstacles we perceive and the instrumental behavior we need to take to overcome the obstacle. The association in turn explains actual, observable changes in behavior. If Joni were to do mental contrasting, her mind would move to the steps she needs to take to overcome her obstacle. It would do this without requiring special thought or attention on her part, at least until she achieved her goal. If Joni happened to then actually run into friends who were planning to attend the party and who encouraged her to do so, she would be more inclined to overcome her obstacle by leaving the party early or even expressing her regrets that she could not attend. And she would be more likely as a result to do well on the exam.

To test this hypothesis, Andreas Kappes and I constructed an experiment that enabled us to observe people's instrumental behavior in a laboratory setting. Asking ninety-nine students to participate, we informed them that college life takes a toll on students' health, but that the World Health Organization had found that students who exercised a half hour more each day could get into better shape.[6] Certain behaviors, such as taking the elevator, could prevent students from getting the exercise they needed to get more fit. "Students just like you," we told the students, "who manage to *exercise* by taking the stairs on a daily basis, report feeling much fitter." Hence we introduced not merely the wish of getting into shape, but an obstacle (taking the elevator) and an instrumental behavior (getting more exercise by taking the stairs when you can).

We proceeded as we had in previous studies, measuring how likely students thought it was that they would become more fit and then having some students perform mental contrasting and others in a control group perform reverse contrasting. Students then undertook the same primed lexical decision task as described earlier, incorporating words related to the obstacle (i.e., elevator) and instrumental behavior (i.e., exercise). Next we measured what participants did when they actually encountered the obstacle of the elevator. We asked them to please go three floors down to have their body mass index (BMI) measured. They could take either the stairs or use an elevator, both located directly opposite the room in which we had been conducting the experiment. As participants left the room, the door closed behind them, leaving them on their own to decide what to do. The students proceeded down to the BMI measurement room, finding a handwritten note that read: "The BMI measurement is cancelled!" Students then came back up to the room where they had begun the experiment, whereupon we debriefed them and thanked them for their participation. We used a hidden camera to record whether they took the stairs on the way down and back up.

As predicted, students who had mentally contrasted and who thought they would become more fit exhibited a strong cognitive association between the obstacle of the elevator and the instrumental behavior of exercise (i.e., their response times in the reaction time tests using these words were shorter). Those who didn't see fitness as a viable wish exhibited a weak cognitive association. In the reverse contrasting group, there was no relationship between the strength of the cognitive association and expectations of future success. When we looked at students' actual behavior, we found that the more optimistic mental contrasting students felt about becoming fit, the more they used the stairs. No such relation was found in students of the control group. Analysis determined that the strength of the cognitive association between the reality and the instrumental behavior was at least partially responsible for frequency of stair use (see fig. 7).

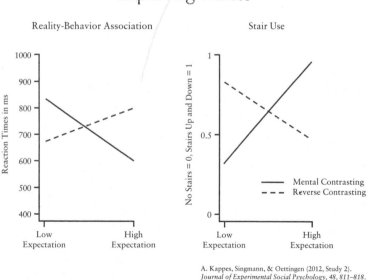

Reality-Behavior Association Improving Fitness

A. Kappes, Singmann, & Oettingen (2012, Study 2).
Journal of Experimental Social Psychology, 48, 811–818.

Figure 7. The higher their expectations of success, the stronger mental contrasting participants' cognitive associations between reality and instrumental behavior (left) and the more their use of stairs (right). This pattern of results did not emerge in participants of the reverse contrasting group.

Chess, Anyone?

Let's back up a minute. Joni, who wants to ace that philosophy exam so badly, is quick to see the big party she's invited to as an obstacle to her wish. In her mind, beer + friends + staying up too late = academic disaster. But Joni, remember, is a strong student in philosophy. Her classmate Kelly, a straight-A student, is an agricultural economics major who signed up for a philosophy minor on a whim. Loaded down with agricultural economics courses, she had wanted to take an easy class with little reading and a professor who didn't give grades lower than B's. She heard that Philosophy 101 was that class. Boy, did she hear wrong. So now Kelly is stuck. With so much of her time taken up by her other classes, she didn't have a chance to read Rousseau's *The Social Contract* that carefully. Hegel's *Phenomenology of Spirit* might as well have been written in ancient Sanskrit. Basically, she won't do well on this exam, no matter how hard she studies in the short window of time available. For her, the party is not an obstacle to getting a good grade, because she can't get a good grade. She might as well hit the party, pound some beers with her buddies, and chow down on some greasy sweet-and-sour chicken at a late-night Chinese dive. If she feels hungover on Sunday, who cares? It's college, she took her agricultural economics exams the day before, and the makeup philosophy exam that the professor offered is in three weeks.

Beyond the effects on nonconscious associations we've already examined, I also thought mental contrasting would work by *affecting the meaning of a reality as an obstacle* in people's conscious and nonconscious minds. When people like Joni performed mental contrasting, their present reality would appear more negative and would be more readily perceptible as an obstacle. For people like Kelly, mental contrasting would make the present reality seem more positive and less of an obstacle. Since part of this cognitive process was happening nonconsciously, the reality's altered meaning would nudge people toward or away from their wishes without any consciously directed effort on their part.

When Andreas Kappes and I asked 130 students to rate how likely they felt it was that they'd get the grade they wanted in a certain class,[7] we had some perform mental contrasting and others either perform reverse contrasting or dwell on the reality standing in the way of making the grade. Afterward, we simply asked the students to rate how pleasant the present reality (the obstacle to their wish) felt to them. We also measured how much students prepared for the final exam in the class. Several days before the exam, we sent an e-mail querying students about how intensely they had studied, how much effort they had put in, and how focused they felt they were during the exam.

Students in the mental contrasting group saw the reality standing in the way of the exam far more negatively if they were optimistic about doing well and less negatively if they weren't optimistic. For students in the other groups, the meaning of the reality didn't change significantly. The students in the mental contrasting group took more or less action to prepare for the exam depending on how likely they felt at the outset that they would succeed. Students in the other groups took action independently of their expectations—not the best approach to achieving a viable wish. A statistical analysis we performed showed that the shift in meaning of the reality was at least partially responsible for actions students took to prepare for the exam. Mental contrasting had worked on the minds of the students who performed it, producing again a tangible result.

Isn't mental contrasting simply reminding participants of the wish, the obstacle, and, implicitly, the means to overcome the obstacle? Wouldn't any process that involved elaboration of the future wish and the present reality lead people to be more aware of the behavior required to achieve their wishes? Our findings suggest otherwise. In reverse contrasting, participants are also being reminded of the wish, the obstacle, and, implicitly, the instrumental behavior. But in students who reverse contrasted, the meaning of the reality did not change as students were more confident they could attain their wishes.

It's compelling that students explicitly said that they perceived their present reality more or less negatively after performing mental contrasting. We were also able to observe this shift in meaning occurring on a nonconscious level. In a separate study, we had students perform what researchers call a "task switching exercise."[8] This experimental procedure is quite complicated to explain; suffice it to say that it is a categorization task that allows researchers to measure minute differences in how quickly people interpret incoming information. We asked 119 students to indicate the graduate school they wanted to attend and how likely they thought they were to attend it. We established three groups: some students performed mental contrasting, some reverse contrasting, and some a dummy exercise. Then we had students perform the task switching exercise on a computer, allowing us to determine whether they could nonconsciously identify the reality as an obstacle. We measured how intensely students were pursuing their goals by asking them to rate how much they felt that external circumstances rather than their own efforts determined their admission to graduate school.

We found once again that mental contrasting worked on participants' nonconscious minds. Students who had mentally contrasted perceived their present realities more identifiably as an obstacle if they thought they were more likely to get into graduate school. They perceived their present realities less sharply as an obstacle if they felt they were less likely to get into graduate school. Ultimately, the tendency of students to regard their realities as obstacles accounted at least partially for how intensely they pursued their goals. Students in the mental contrasting group who saw present realities more sharply as obstacles expressed a greater sense of responsibility for whether they would get into graduate school, and those who saw present realities less sharply as obstacles were less inclined to take personal responsibility for achieving this wish. Mental contrasting thus shaped participants' view of reality, helping them become more aware of the elements standing in their way, and in the process leading them to feel more strongly about pursuing a wish.

Joni might see the party more sharply as an obstacle thanks to mental contrasting, but get this: she would also be more inclined to recognize a new obstacle to her wishes when it presented itself. We asked sixty-five children at six German chess clubs to indicate how long they had been playing chess at the club, and we gauged from initial tests how competent they were at the game. We then told the children that we would reward them for their participation by enrolling them in a lottery in which they could win some cool chess computer games.[9] The faster they succeeded in the chess tasks we gave them, the more tickets to the lottery they'd receive. In response to our queries, the children told us how many tickets they'd like to win, and they also rated how likely they felt they were to win them. Some of the children then performed mental contrasting around the wish of winning tickets, the rest reverse contrasting.

The children then all performed two tasks. In the first, the "obstacle" task, they had to detect that their own queen blocked them from achieving checkmate. We assigned them white chess pieces, and to win they had to realize that two moves were required, the first being movement of their queen. In the second, "non-obstacle" task, we assigned the children the black pieces and asked them to figure out how to trap their opponent's king. Neither the children's pieces nor those of their opponents physically blocked a checkmate, and the children could win by making three moves. Having pretested both of these tasks, we knew that they were of equal difficulty for the children, even though the second task involved three moves and the first only two (see fig. 8).

In analyzing our results, we made sure to adjust statistically for children's different skill levels at chess. We found that children who had performed mental contrasting were more likely to detect their own piece as an obstacle that prevented

Chess Tasks

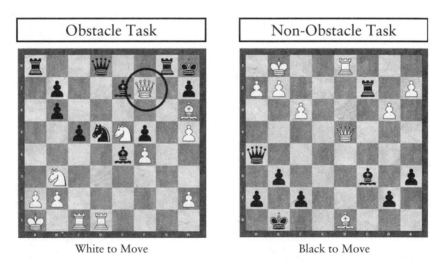

Figure 8. The two chess tasks that all children were asked to solve.

checkmate if they had initially thought winning the lottery tickets was feasible, and less likely if they had initially doubted their ability to win the lottery tickets. When it came to the non-obstacle tasks, students in the mental contrasting group performed about the same as those in the control group. Mental contrasting enhanced children's ability to detect obstacles in their path when they were pursuing a viable wish, and it decreased their abilities to detect obstacles when the wish in question wasn't viable. Children who performed mental contrasting were thus better equipped to pursue their goals and to handle the unanticipated obstacles that could crop up.

> *Focus on a wish you think you will probably achieve but that is challenging for you. Take a few minutes to perform mental contrasting with that wish. Now let a week or two pass. Sit down with a notebook and list all the additional obstacles that got in your way that you were able to perceive and overcome. How many were there? If your wish was to exercise more after work, and the obstacle you initially came up with was wanting to spend time relaxing in front of the TV, did you also find yourself passing up other opportunities to relax—such as when a friend invited you out for dinner, or when you happened to see an interesting magazine lying on the table in your home that just beckoned to be read?*

You Might Want to Improve . . .

So far, I've explained the benefits of mental contrasting by showing how this short and simple exercise affects people's conscious thought and nonconscious perception of reality. But mental contrasting also works on an entirely different level to help people pursue and attain their wishes. One reason Joni might achieve her wish of doing well on her philosophy exam is that she is better at responding to the negative feedback of her professor, her peers, and others. Previous research has shown that people who are pursuing goals benefit from negative feedback, since it allows them to adjust their behavior and do what they need to do to acquire new skills.[10] Yet depending on what it is and how it is given, negative feedback can be hard to handle, threatening the way individuals see themselves, affecting their beliefs in their own competences, and sometimes making their wishes seem out of their grasp. People tend to forget negative feedback, even when it is trivial, and remember instead the affirming things others say about them.[11] In some cases, people who receive negative feedback tend to lose heart and pursue their wishes less energetically.

I wondered whether mental contrasting would shelter people from losing heart when receiving negative feedback, or, even better, help them make use of the constructive information negative feedback may contain. In a first study, my collaborators and I asked 153 students to identify an important interpersonal wish or concern, such as getting along better with a boyfriend or getting acquainted with roommates.[12] Asking them how likely they thought they were to achieve this wish, we had some students perform mental contrasting around the wish, some indulge in the future, and others dwell on the present reality standing in the way. During the second part of the experiment, students received a test on a computer that supposedly measured social competence. As part of the test (which was drawn from a test previously developed by psychologists),[13] students responded to a series of pictures. They looked at an image of a woman (see fig. 9) and tried to pin down her salient personality traits; they looked at a landscape and indicated how it made them feel; they looked at a picture of a hugging couple and told us how long they thought the couple had been together; and they looked at a picture of a man near an open window and explained what they thought he would do in the next five minutes.

Students received feedback based on their alleged perform-ance on the test. Twelve feedback statements flashed on the screen before them, including some that depicted a weakness in specific social situations (e.g., "In socially challenging situations, you feel overwhelmed") and others that depicted a strength (e.g., "In interpersonal relationships, you are open-minded"). We asked students to study this list of feedback statements they'd re-ceived. Afterward, we asked them to recall portions of individual

Picture Test to Create Feedback

Please look at this picture for a minute.
Then answer—without much thought—the following question:

What are the characteristics of this woman?
Please circle the appropriate dot on each of the lines below.

warm	⌐ ⌐ ⌐ ⌐ ⌐ ⌐ ⌐ ⌐	cold
fragile	⌐ ⌐ ⌐ ⌐ ⌐ ⌐ ⌐ ⌐	strong
passive	⌐ ⌐ ⌐ ⌐ ⌐ ⌐ ⌐ ⌐	active
impatient	⌐ ⌐ ⌐ ⌐ ⌐ ⌐ ⌐ ⌐	patient
dependent	⌐ ⌐ ⌐ ⌐ ⌐ ⌐ ⌐ ⌐	independent
jealous	⌐ ⌐ ⌐ ⌐ ⌐ ⌐ ⌐ ⌐	faithful

Figure 9. An example of a picture students had to respond to.

statements; for instance, we cued them with, "In socially challenging situations, you feel . . ." and they had to fill in the adjective.

Students who had performed mental contrasting recalled significantly more of the negative feedback items that we gave them when they had high expectations of achieving their interpersonal wishes and fewer when they had low expectations. Students who had indulged or dwelled remembered a middling amount of negative feedback items, regardless of whether they expected to succeed or not. All the students remembered the positive feedback (see fig. 10). Mental contrasting thus helped students better process the negative feedback relating to their specified goals.

Recall of Negative and Positive Feedback

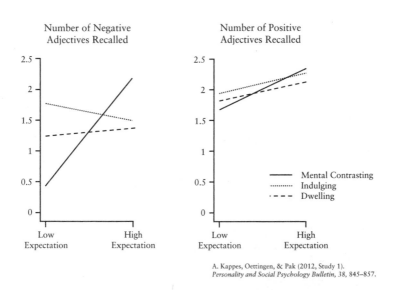

A. Kappes, Oettingen, & Pak (2012, Study 1).
Personality and Social Psychology Bulletin, 38, 845–857.

Figure 10. The higher their expectations of success, the more negative feedback adjectives mental contrasting participants recalled (left). This pattern of results did not emerge in indulging and dwelling participants. No expectancy-dependent recall was observed for positive feedback adjectives in either condition (right).

Similar experiments confirmed how helpful mental contrasting was in the processing of negative feedback. When students performed mental contrasting, they were better able to hear negative feedback and translate it into effective plans for realizing their wishes. They also had higher self-esteem, seeing themselves as more competent than participants in the control groups. They perceived negative feedback constructively as identifying a deficit that could be mastered in the future, that was restricted to the given situation, and that was repairable through effort. Meanwhile, mental contrasting made negative feedback harder to take when success wasn't likely, further nudging individuals to let go of these unrealistic dreams and move on to something more promising.

Use Your Whole Mind

One of my friends, Brenda, recently performed mental contrasting. Her wish, she told me, was to get back in the habit of daily exercise. When she was younger, she used to exercise a lot, but now she hardly ever did. When I asked her about the obstacle that prevented her from exercising every day, she told me "laziness, not wanting to put the time and effort into doing it for an hour or two. I think it's mostly laziness, just not being able to get up and do it."

"Why don't you want to put in the effort?" I asked. "In other areas of life, you push really hard."

She thought for a moment. "When I was exercising before, I wound up hating it and so I stopped. I think now it's just me having a past dislike of it from doing it so often. . . . I can't get over the fact of having a kind of stigma against doing it."

I probed deeper, asking her why she used to hate it so much.

She replied that when she was younger she had an eating disorder that compelled her to exercise all the time, beyond the point of exhaustion. She would do it even though she hated it. It was a shame because before her eating disorder took control, Brenda had very much enjoyed athletics. Now just going into a gym brought up painful memories of a difficult time in her life, a time when she had pushed herself to go beyond her body's inherent capacities.

While she was imagining the obstacle, Brenda slowly opened her eyes. Her face brightened. "Oh," she exclaimed, "I just realized something. I can overcome my laziness and my hatred of exercising. All I need to do is understand that I'm not in the same place as I was back then. I'm emotionally more stable than I was before, and now I can control whether I exercise or not." Brenda simply needed to remind herself that exercise was "not something that I have to do," but something that "I want to do." She was free now to exercise as long as she was feeling like it, but no longer.

Discoveries, insights, revelations—these happen to people during and immediately after mental contrasting. As this chapter has argued, mental contrasting creates powerful changes in people, affecting how they perceive reality and how they respond to the feedback others give. New associations form in people's minds, near-instant connections between dream and obstacle, between obstacle and the means of overcoming the obstacle. All of a sudden, in ways that can scarcely be put into words, the obstacle seems more clearly defined than it did before. That's the "magic" of mental contrasting, explaining why such a short mental exercise, accessible to anyone who is open to it, young or old, from all walks of life, can prove so powerful as a self-regulatory strategy for fulfilling wishes and addressing concerns of all kinds.

We're used to exerting conscious effort to achieve our goals—to push hard, to strive. There is nothing wrong, of course, with doing that. But as Brenda and others in our experiments will tell you, you can accomplish so much more, direct your energies better, and pursue what really matters to you and what you realistically can achieve by moving beyond the conscious and the rational. Dreaming a little and then imagining the obstacle lets you unlock new potentials inside yourself, potentials you scarcely knew existed. Until now, you have likely approached life using only part of your mind's latent capacities. Mental contrasting lets you finally engage in viable, heartfelt wishes with everything you've got.

Chapter Six

. . . .

The Magic of WOOP

In the fall of 2013, I traveled to Minnesota to work with groups of school counselors employed by the Minnesota Office of Higher Education. A member of one group, a middle-aged woman named Tammy, told me of a problem she was having in her daily life. She came home after working a full day and then felt overwhelmed by all the chores she had to do, such as making dinner, doing laundry, grocery shopping, and paying bills. With so much on her plate, she would forget to have fun, and her relationships with her kids and her husband were suffering. She wanted to come home at night and find a way to spend time with her family rather than becoming a servant to her to-do list.

Tammy tried mental contrasting and framed her wish for the next twenty-four hours: She wanted to come home from work and enjoy her evening without getting overwhelmed. The best future outcome that Tammy fantasized about was that she would feel harmony and a sense of belongingness as her family enjoyed a home-cooked meal together. Furthermore, she imagined having additional time to spend bonding with her kids and husband. Tammy listed as an obstacle the many things she needed to do around the house. Looking more deeply inward, she realized that the obstacle was really the pressure she put on herself to get everything done. Her plan to overcome the obstacle was simple: if she started to feel stressed by the overwhelming tasks, she would remind herself that she wanted to prioritize closeness with her family. She would either let some tasks go or resolve to do them another time.

The next day, Tammy reported how it went. When she got home, as usual, she was slammed by chores. However, the exercise she had performed helped put her onto a different path. When she started to feel the usual pressure upon coming home, she switched into gear and began preparing a homey dinner. With the smell of pot roast filling the house, her son and husband wandered hungrily into the kitchen, and soon all three sat talking at the dinner table—something they had not done in quite a while. Although Tammy had to clean the kitchen after dinner and help her son with his homework, she resolved to let the laundry go and do it over the weekend. With the time she saved, she baked chocolate chip cookies that the whole family enjoyed. She was also able to go on an hour-long walk with her husband. As Tammy related, she had been able to better prioritize how to spend her time, rather than focusing on one thing—her chores—at the expense of all else. To her surprise, the chores themselves took on new meaning. Cleaning the kitchen didn't seem quite as burdensome as it usually did, possibly because she was enjoying other parts of her evening.

Another woman in the group, Leslie, had a different kind of twenty-four-hour wish. Her puppy Jo-Jo needed to sleep in his crate, because if he didn't, he barked all night, which prevented Leslie from getting a decent night's sleep. This wasn't all Jo-Jo's fault: Leslie neglected to give him enough exercise during the day, so when night came, he was too antsy to go into his crate. If getting a good night's sleep was Leslie's wish, the desired outcome she imagined was feeling calm, rested, and strong at work the next day. The obstacle, Leslie discovered, was her own sense of being too busy to take a walk with Jo-Jo. Her plan went like this: if I feel too busy to take a walk, I will remind myself how much Jo-Jo will benefit from taking a walk and I'll take him out anyway.

The next day, Leslie reported good news: She had taken Jo-Jo for a walk, and he had gone into his crate with his tail wagging. Leslie had gone straight to bed and gotten eight solid hours of sound sleep, more than she had in weeks.

Mental contrasting doesn't just help people pursue feasible wishes in a laboratory setting. Anyone can use it as a tool to master all sorts of real-life problems and challenges. Mental contrasting can be taught as what psychologists call a "meta-cognitive" strategy—a strategy that provides people with knowledge or awareness of their own thoughts and mental images.[1] Using mental contrasting, Tammy could observe herself and understand that her own anxiety about "getting it all done" was preventing her from having fun and being close with her family. She could further understand how to handle this anxiety when it reared its ugly head. Likewise, Leslie could frame a wish for herself—getting a good night's sleep—and understand that she was getting in her own way of achieving her goal. She could become more aware of her patterns of thinking and thereby make behavior changes that improved her life.

It might seem obvious that mental contrasting would help people pursue feasible wishes, given the research I've presented so far. Yet phenomena observed under strictly controlled laboratory conditions sometimes aren't observed under the more diverse and unpredictable circumstances of the real world. The gap between basic science and lay applications of science can still be huge; you can observe this by simply opening up a scientific journal and trying to parse through the obtuse language and statistical terms. In the case of mental contrasting, we didn't know if people would readily learn this exercise and deploy it on their own to address their problems. It turned out that they did—with results every bit as compelling as those we'd seen in our laboratory experiments. We also discovered that introducing a new element—the formulation of an explicit plan in case the obstacle was encountered—made mental contrasting work even better than it had been on its own. Thus the laboratory magic of mental contrasting was translated into real-life magic.

Taking It to the Streets

Our transformation of mental contrasting into a tool for real-life use unfolded gradually over several years. During the early 1990s, when I first began working with mental contrasting, I was not focused on its practical applications; I had little professional experience with clinical therapy, counseling, or testing—the ways psychology is most commonly applied. I began my career as a biologist doing basic research, and as I moved into psychology, the experiments I created remained theoretical, re-flecting a predominantly intellectual desire to understand why positive fantasies lowered performance, whether mental contrasting would work better, and how exactly mental contrasting worked. My students and I went where the data took us without knowing whether what we had found would ever turn out to better people's lives.

As time passed and we saw research participants do well with mental contrasting, I came to think that many more people could benefit from using it as a behavior regulation tool. I also was seeing people at work as well as acquaintances and friends trying and failing to make progress in their lives by "thinking positive" and ignoring the obstacles. Individuals trying to stay healthy would imagine their bodies free of disease, while others whose kids were acting out would try to get them to behave better by fantasizing about their great behavior. Positive thinking was another "metacognitive" tool, perhaps the most dominant one in popular culture, yet it didn't seem to be working all too well nor was it rooted in scientific evidence.

My collaborators and I conducted an initial study in which we explored if we could teach mental contrasting and have people apply it profitably in their everyday lives and to whatever wishes or concerns they might have.[2] We recruited fifty-two midlevel managers in the health care field ranging from twenty-six to fifty-nine years old. Executives rising up in health care typically have stressful jobs that require them to manage their resources carefully. Department heads are holding them accountable for delivering superior performance; subordinates are making requests that often conflict with company policies. It's plain to see why being in the middle of that hierarchy would prevent executives from enjoying much authority in their jobs.

Poor communication, disorganized work environments, and long hours also leave them emotionally exhausted and sometimes physically ill. Many workers today are stressed out, but we thought midlevel health care executives would especially appreciate a strategy that helped them deal with their jam-packed, emotionally challenging lives.

We told participants that we were investigating "free thoughts and images in everyday life." Participants began by naming their presently most important personal problem—like being in conflict with an employee, having to write a business report, or having to design a proposal. They then listed four words or phrases associated with achieving their respective wishes and four that captured obstacles impeding a happy ending. On a large blank sheet of paper, participants were asked to write inside thought bubbles. One group was taught to use these to mentally contrast, another to indulge only in their positive fantasies. We then had participants generate as many important everyday problems as they could from their personal as well as professional lives. Participants either mentally contrasted or indulged about wishes arising from the first six of the problems, the first one in writing and the last five in their minds. We gave participants a booklet for them to write in over the next two weeks. Each day, participants had to write down a problem they were most worried about that day and either mentally contrast or indulge around that problem in writing. For any other problems or wishes they might have for the day, they were asked to perform mental contrasting or indulging in their minds when they had a chance, such as while waiting in line at the supermarket.

Two weeks later, we asked participants to fill out a follow-up questionnaire. We asked them how successful they were in organizing their time, how many tasks or projects they gave up, how many long-overdue projects they finished during the previous two weeks, and how easy they found it to make decisions. Participants who had mentally contrasted reported having been more successful at managing their time and also at selectively completing projects. They also had less trouble making decisions. We concluded that mental contrasting was a useful tool—and also a cost- and time-effective one—that people could use to manage their everyday lives.[3]

In this last study, mental contrasting enabled participants to better allocate their scarce time because it helped them choose which wishes to pursue and which to leave behind. We wondered whether mental contrasting would work in a group setting where individuals were looking to succeed at a task and where letting go was not an option. In an investigation led by my son Anton, we went to a public elementary school located in a low-income neighborhood in Germany and taught forty-nine second- and third-grade students to either mentally contrast or indulge about successfully completing a language assignment and winning a bag of candy.[4] We told the students that they would have two weeks to study fifteen cartoons with a corresponding English vocabulary word. At the end of two weeks, they would take a quiz in which they'd write the English word under the corresponding picture. Any second grader who got four or more words right or third grader who got seven or more words right would win the candy.

With the children now excited to participate, we gave them each a booklet to fill out. First they told us how sure they were that they'd win the candy and how much they wanted to win it. Half the students then wrote about "the best thing" and the "second best thing" that would happen if they won the prize.

The other half of the students, those who performed mental contrasting, wrote about the best thing as well, but instead of continuing to the second best thing, they imagined what behavior of theirs could prevent them from winning the prize.

Two days later, we gave the children ten of the fifteen English words. A week after our initial intervention, we provided the remaining five words as well as study kits containing blank pieces of paper. Coordinating with the teachers, we chose English words that were easy enough so the children could learn them if they put in moderate effort (e.g., "train," "car," "happy," "sad"). Two weeks later, students took the quiz and all students received candy.

Since the task was feasible for all students and was also a new task around which students hadn't generated previous expectations of success, we predicted that mental contrasting would improve performance across the board. Our results bore that out. Students who performed mental contrasting did better on the test than those who only fantasized about their success. A similar experiment with fifth graders from low-income backgrounds in the United States turned up the same results. The findings suggested that teachers in schools could use mental contrasting to improve students' performance on new, viable tasks. Since schools commonly exhort students only to "stay positive" and dream about future possibilities, educators stood to gain from modifying that message by helping children imagine the obstacles as well.

A number of other studies we've conducted have confirmed the usefulness of mental contrasting as a self-regulation tool. They've also revealed a surprising phenomenon: mental contrasting around a given wish can create energizing effects that carry over to wishes in other domains. In one study, we induced mental contrasting in one group of students around the wish of doing well on an intelligence test. Other students in the study either indulged in positive fantasies or performed a dummy procedure. The students who mentally contrasted and expected to do well on the test showed increases in systolic blood pressure, suggesting that they had become energized. But they also tried harder at a letter writing exercise we gave them. In a separate study, we found that mental contrasting around the wish of "writing an excellent essay" helped participants devote more energy to squeezing a handgrip. Used as a tool, mental contrasting around feasible wishes seems to lead to a more general increase in people's engagement.[5] This increase in engagement can leach over into areas where people don't feel confident about succeeding. By mentally contrasting in an area where you're strong, you can increase your odds of succeeding even in areas where you're weak. For instance, a person who performs mental contrasting around a wish of having a nice evening with his wife can also increase his odds that afternoon of writing a difficult e-mail he had long neglected.

Giving Mental Contrasting a Boost

Despite how promising mental contrasting seemed to be as a practical tool, I couldn't help but wonder if there was a way we could make it work even more effectively. During the 1990s, as I was experimenting with mental contrasting, my husband, Peter M. Gollwitzer, was pursuing fascinating research of his own in a related area. He was studying a concept that he called "implementation intentions,"[6] the forging of explicit intentions about *how* to achieve a wish. If you break down the process by which people pursue wishes, you can distinguish two phases: an initial phase in which you weigh your options and decide to commit to a goal, and a second phase in which you plan how to take action to attain the wish. Decades of research had shown that strongly intending to pursue a wish can improve the chances that the wish will be realized. If Jim, a salesperson, wants to improve his relationship with his regional manager, and his colleague Colleen is only somewhat interested in doing so, Jim stands a marginally better chance of improving the relationship. Experiments show that a person's intentions only slightly boost performance.[7] Jim might want to improve his relationship with his regional manager, but all kinds of factors—difficulty getting started, for instance, or the presence of distractions—might intercede to prevent Jim from taking meaningful action.

Peter and his collaborator, Veronika Brandstätter, found that once we've firmly committed to achieving a goal, explicitly formulating a plan for attaining that goal could help people take action and overcome obstacles. In one early study of university students, they set a difficult task for participants: write a report two days after Christmas Eve about how they spent their holidays.[8] Half the group was asked to specify where, when, and how they were going to write the report (in other words, make an exact plan) while the other half was not asked to specify. Of the participants who made a plan as to when, where, and how they would act, 71 percent sent the report back in to the researchers. Of participants who hadn't formed a plan, only 32 percent sent back a report. The simple act of making a plan was serving as a self-regulatory tool, playing a profound role in helping people follow through on their goals.

As time passed and Peter conducted more studies, he came to realize that forming a plan for how to attain a certain goal—what he termed the "implementation intention"—had a more powerful effect if it took on the particular form of an "if-then" statement: "If situation x arises, then I will perform response y." Let's suppose Jim feels inexplicably anxious when his regional manager stops by the office, so it's difficult for Jim to start up a conversation or ask a question. Jim's implementation intention might be "If I become nervous talking to my regional manager, then I will remind myself that I'm the top-performing salesperson in the district and my sales have increased since last year"; or "If I become nervous talking to my regional manager, then I will excuse myself for a moment, take a few deep breaths to calm down, and return to the conversation."

Since the early 1990s, Peter and others have performed many dozens of experiments examining the effects of implementation intentions with goals as diverse as using public transportation, eating a low-fat diet, completing a reading assignment, following New Year's resolutions, performing testicular self-examinations to detect cancer, and attending workplace safety training. Statistical analysis of almost one hundred of these studies found that implementation intentions had a "medium-to-large" impact on actual behavior, significantly increasing the likelihood that people would achieve their goals. Implementation intentions helped people get started on tasks, "whether getting started was an issue of remembering to act, seizing good opportunities, or overcoming initial reluctance." It also helped people protect against distractions, overcome counterproductive but habitual behaviors, and retain the energy to tackle new goals once the goal at hand has been achieved.[9]

Implementation intentions were shown to work especially well with people who had trouble controlling their actions. In one study of twenty drug addicts experiencing withdrawal symptoms, Peter and his colleagues asked one group to frame implementation intentions around the accepted goal of writing a short résumé before 5 p.m. that day (hospital staff encouraged the addicts to write résumés so they might find work upon their release from treatment).[10] Another group expressed the same intention to write the résumé but didn't have to specify a plan for where or when they would write. At 5 p.m., eight of the ten addicts who had formed implementation intentions had written their résumés. Of the ten addicts who hadn't framed a prior plan, none had done so.

How can something as simple as forming an "if *situation*, then *behavior*" statement do so much to plug the gap between intentions and behavior, helping people perform better? Like mental contrasting, implementation intentions seemingly work magic by operating on an automatic or nonconscious level.[11] In fact, forming implementation intentions prepares us mentally to take action by preactivating in our minds the situation of an obstacle or opportunity arising. Jim, the salesman who wishes to improve his relationship with his boss, becomes cued in to the appearance of the obstacle—in this case, the onset of anxiety—and is able to react quickly. He easily notices the anxiety creeping up and readily responds to it as planned. The situational cue of the anxiety does the work of controlling his behavior, causing it to happen immediately, as if by reflex. Instead of searching for opportunities to take action, he has a hard time *not* acting once the anxiety creeps up. He's not making a conscious decision to act—he just does it when triggered. Implementation intentions thus *supplement* any conscious effort we might be making to achieve a goal. Like mental contrasting, it programs our own automatic selves to respond in a helpful way, allowing us to regulate our behavior better.

In discussing our work together, Peter and I sensed that

mental contrasting and implementation intentions would complement each other as a metacognitive strategy. We've seen that mental contrasting prepares you cognitively to pursue wishes by linking the future and the obstacles in your mind. How much better off might you be if you were also explicitly engaging your mind to respond in predetermined ways to the specified obstacles once they occur? In addition, mental contrasting gets people focused and committed to a wish—the precondition for implementation intentions to work.[12] Performing mental contrasting and implementation intentions together—what we at first somewhat inelegantly termed MCII—could make selecting and attaining wishes easier and more effective by maximizing the work your mind does without your conscious effort. As a practical strategy for handling daily life, MCII could enable you to put all of yourself behind your wishes, regulating your behavior so you can more effectively engage with the world around you.

Think about how hard it is to follow through on intentions once you form them. You might resolve to cut out sweets for a couple of months to lose weight, yet it's a colleague's birthday and someone plops a luscious Boston cream pie onto the conference table at a meeting. In that situation, you might remember your diet and consciously resist a slice of pie, but what happens if you're tired or stressed? What happens if someone plops the cream pie down at the precise moment in the late afternoon when you're used to having a little treat? Just adopting a conscious wish and making conscious effort will help you some of the time, but in critical situations when obstacles appear, it's hard to stay on track. You need something extra, something nonconscious, something like implementation intentions. But keep in mind that these critical situations are exactly what people become tuned into when they are performing mental contrasting. As we saw in chapter 5, mental contrasting also fixes a nonconscious link in your mind between obstacles and the behavior required to overcome them. You can now see why mental contrasting and implementation intentions seemed like such a natural combination, potentially much more effective than performing either mental contrasting or implementation intentions alone. You're preparing your mind to identify and respond automatically and efficiently to obstacles in your path right at the moment they first appear.

Was the double action of MCII really more effective? To find out, we wandered a bit more deeply into the realm of Boston cream pies, performing an experiment involving female undergraduate students who were trying to change an unhealthy snacking habit. Marieke Adriaanse, Peter, and I asked participants to tell us their most unhealthy snacking habit, one they felt they would be able to change over the following week, albeit with some difficulty.[13] We asked them how viable it would be for them to cut back on this particular food or drink and how important it would be for them to do so. Some participants performed mental contrasting around the wish, some only formed implementation intentions (if *obstacle x* arises, then I will perform *behavior y*), and some did both mental contrasting and implementation intentions.

We asked participants to perform that same mental exercise each morning upon awakening. A week later we checked in with them, administering a questionnaire. In addition to asking how successful they felt they were at cutting back on their unhealthy snacking habit, we asked them how many times they were able *not* to consume the unhealthy food when they had an urge and how many times they consumed the unhealthy food compared with the previous week. They also indicated how much they felt the exercise helped them to think about their bad habit in a different light. Finally, we asked some questions designed to control for factors that might have skewed the results, such as how often participants performed the exercise they had learned in the experiment.

The results were striking. All participants reported making progress in their efforts to control snacking, as we had expected. But participants who performed MCII reported substantially more progress than those who performed mental contrasting or implementation intentions alone (see fig. 11). The success participants experienced did not have to do with how strong their

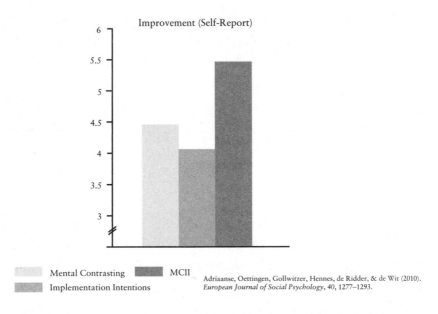

Figure 11. MCII participants reported more progress in breaking their snacking habits than both mental contrasting only and implementation intentions only participants.

habits were initially. Even participants with strong snacking habits made progress. Participants who performed MC, with or without implementation intentions, reported having more clarity about their habits. Those who additionally had formed a plan (i.e., the MCII group) were best able to translate this clarity into tangible performance.

Introducing WOOP

As I started to teach mental contrasting with implementation intentions as a single, unified tool, I realized that we needed a better name than "MCII." The name WOOP—Wish, Outcome, Obstacle, Plan—came to us almost by accident in the course of fielding a study. We liked how accessible WOOP was and how well it captured the key steps. As a tool, WOOP is what psychologists call "content neutral," that is, it can be used to help with any kind of wish you might have, short term or long term, big or small. If you're a professional, you can use it to reach a new milestone in your career, improve your skills—whatever you can think of. If you're a student, you can apply it to study more productively. If you're a mom or dad, you can apply it to handle challenging situations with your children more effectively. Anyone can use it in his or her personal life for any purpose—for instance, to form closer relationships with others or to improve health.

I'll offer some suggestions on how best to apply WOOP in chapter 8, but for now I'd like to take you through the exercise in a bit more detail—the same exercise that the two women at the beginning of this chapter used to achieve meaningful behavior change in their everyday lives in a mere twenty-four hours.

First of all, remember that WOOP is different from other exercises you may have tried in that it involves free thoughts and images rather than rational or effortful thinking. You need to focus so that the thoughts and images will flow. Find a secluded place where you can enjoy some peace and quiet. Make yourself comfortable so that you can focus. What a relief it is to put away your electronic devices and separate yourself from the hustle and bustle of normal life. If you can't find mental space to perform WOOP because you are involved in another task, finish your task first and then do WOOP. If this is your first time, fifteen to twenty minutes should be enough time for the exercise. As you become more familiar with WOOP, you will be able to create your mental space and do it much more quickly— in a matter of a few minutes or even less.

We begin with the "W" in WOOP, a wish or concern that you might have. Relax, take another breath, and think about one wish or concern in your personal or professional life, something that is challenging but that you think is possible for you to achieve in a given period of time. It could be something you could accomplish in a year, a month, a week, a day—whatever wish you decide to WOOP. If you have several wishes for the same time period, pick the one that is most important to you. Put the wish or concern in your mind's eye and hold it there.

Now think of the first "O" in WOOP, the outcome. What is the best thing that you associate with fulfilling your wish or solving your concern? Identify this outcome and keep it in your mind's eye. Really think about it; imagine the relevant events and experiences as vividly as possible. Let your mind go. Don't hesitate to give your thoughts and images free rein. Take your time; you may close your eyes if you would like.

When you are ready, open your eyes again. It's time to focus on the second "O" in WOOP, the obstacle. Sometimes things do not work out as well as we would like. What is it in you that holds you back? What is it really? Find the most critical, internal obstacle that prevents you from fulfilling your wish or solving your concern. What thoughts or behaviors might play a role? How about habits or preconceived notions? When thinking about obstacles, people often look to the external world, naming circumstances or individuals they feel are blocking them. But by choosing a wish that we think is feasible, we're already accounting for obstacles outside us (if serious obstacles outside us existed, the wish wouldn't be feasible). The point of this exercise is to help us prevent ourselves from getting in the way of realizing our own dreams.

In selecting an internal obstacle, it's also important to dig deep enough to make sure you are addressing one that's critical for you. Depending on the situation, this obstacle might be as specific as spending too much time in front of the computer or as general as being tired or being anxious. The obstacle could be a behavior, an emotion, an obsessive thought, an impulse, a bad habit, assumptions you jump to, or just a silly, vain behavior. Sometimes it takes a little bit of thought and patience to really understand your inner barriers and how you behave or react unconstructively. Sticking with the process *can be hard at first since we're so often dissuaded from taking honest looks at ourselves, but finding your most relevant obstacle really pays off. It's not as hard to take as it might seem, and many people find it fulfilling and even quite a relief. In many cases, you'll be discovering something about yourself that you never would have thought or that you had not quite understood before. By finding your obstacle, you'll gain what in German is called* Durchblick, *loosely translated as a new, clearer vista on your wish or concern, or possibly on other aspects of your life. Please keep the obstacle in your mind's eye. Then really think about it. Imagine the relevant events and experiences as vividly as possible. Once again, let your mind go. Do not hesitate to give your thoughts and images free rein. You may close your eyes again if you like.*

When you are ready, let's move to the "P" part of WOOP—the plan. What can you do to overcome or circumvent your obstacle? Name one thought or action you can take—the most effective one—and hold it in your mind. Then think about when and where the obstacle will next occur. Form an if-then plan: "If obstacle x occurs (when and where), then I will perform behavior y." Repeat this if-then plan to yourself one more time.

And that's it. You're done. Wasn't that simple? You can do WOOP as often as you like and in any location where you can create a little mental space for yourself. You can close your eyes and WOOP on the bus, train, or plane, when you are bored, while waiting for your colleagues or friends. Do WOOP every morning or when you go to bed at night. Invent a ritual around WOOP, but also do it opportunistically in stressful situations and in situations where your problem is vague and its solution uncertain.

The version of WOOP we just did together is a mental form. You can also do it in writing.

On a blank sheet of paper, name the wish in three to six words. Identify the best outcome (also in three to six words) and write it down. Now let your thoughts lead your pen, taking as much paper as you need. Then name your obstacle and write it down. Imagine the obstacle, again letting your thoughts wander and lead your writing. To create a plan, first write down one specific action you can take to overcome the obstacle. Write down the time and place when you believe the obstacle will arise. Then write down the if-then plan: "If obstacle x occurs (when and where), then I will perform behavior y." Repeat it once to yourself out loud.

A common mistake in forming if-then plans is keeping the "if-then" structure but substituting other terms for the ones I've specified. For instance, an attorney who wants to behave more assertively in the courtroom might erroneously say, "If I raise my voice and challenge the opposing attorney, then I will help my client succeed." Remember that the plan you're creating is contingent on the appearance of the obstacle or situation: If *obstacle or appropriate situation*, then *goal-directed behavior*. This attorney's plan might better read: "If I feel insecure when the attorney for the other side objects, then I will remind myself that I am just as competent and knowledgeable as she is" or "If I start to panic when the judge questions my argument, then I will remind myself that I have argued before her three times already and she has always found in my favor."

WOOP always works the same, no matter the time frame you're working with or the kind of wish you have. In forming your if-then plans, note that you can also frame plans to *prevent* obstacles, not just surmount or circumvent them when they arise. A student who wants to prevent her obstacle of feeling disengaged at the end of senior year would write her if-then plan as follows: "If I walk into class (situation), then I will focus immediately on the teacher (behavior)." You can also frame if-then plans to take advantage of opportunities to solve your problem. A student who wants to seize every opportunity to work on staying engaged until the end of senior year might have the following plan: "If I go on the Internet this afternoon (situation), then I will search for information about the orientation of the college I wish to attend (behavior).

You can use WOOP in all life circumstances, not only if you are struggling or feel you need improvement. Even good job candidates or strong students can use WOOP to be even more creative and productive, as it can help them overcome any fears of failure they might have or other mental blocks that might impede them from developing to their full potential. Also, the very process of performing WOOP can help anyone adjust his or her wishes. You might find as you perform WOOP that a wish you thought was challenging but attainable is not so attainable after all; as you come face-to-face with the obstacle, it winds up being far more difficult and costlier than you thought. In this way, WOOP is still helping you perform at your best— by helping you disengage from unfeasible wishes and focus on wishes that *are* feasible.

When you embark on a WOOP exercise, you never know what you're going to find. Since people so seldom look obstacles in the face, the experience of doing so is often emotional. Remember the group of Minnesota school counselors I mentioned working with at the beginning of the chapter? One of them was a thirty-year-old man named Colin who told me that his wish was to buy a house with his partner David in the next eighteen months. "I want to finally have a family of my own, including children," Colin said. When I asked him to imagine the outcome, he described having a happy and healthy kid with David and living all together as a functional family.

The obstacle was a little more difficult for Colin to put his finger on. His face grew serious, and he looked away for a long moment before speaking. "The problem, I guess, is that I don't want to associate myself with the family I grew up in—it was just too painful not being accepted for who I was. In buying a house and living a more domestic life, I feel that I would be choosing a similar lifestyle. I also would be committing to living in Minnesota and growing old here. I'm not sure I'm ready for any of this." I asked Colin to choose a single obstacle to work with; he picked the anxiety he feels about living in Minnesota as opposed to a big, exciting city like Chicago. His if-then plan read as follows: "If I start to feel anxious or stressed about living in Minnesota, then I will remind myself that my new family with David is a healthy one and that I benefit from having a network of people here who care about me."

As of this writing, I don't know if Colin has yet realized his wish, but I do know that he left the session clearer about his situation. The ambivalence that he felt had melted away, and he had a plan for how to overcome his internal obstacles. Furthermore, he now has a simple tool at his disposal that he can use daily or even multiple times a day to push closer to achieving his challenging but feasible wish.

What might you learn from using WOOP? Where might WOOP take you? If you're like many people, you've found it hard at times to realize wishes even though they are in your grasp to achieve. Now is your chance to engage your nonconscious mind and get all your energies behind a specific goal. It's your chance to discover what has been holding you back all this time and how to conquer it. It's your chance to connect with the world and with those around you more forcefully than you ever have. What are you waiting for?

Chapter Seven

. . . .

WOOP Your Life

If you're still skeptical about WOOP, you have a right to be. Many popular self-help or "success" books promise readers they'll enjoy better health, foster stronger relationships, find new financial opportunities, or achieve any other wish they might imagine. Also, the very nature of WOOP might make you doubt the technique. WOOP doesn't cost anything to learn, it doesn't involve significant expenditure of time, it doesn't come with harmful side effects, its effects can begin immediately, it does not require working with a trainer or other professional, and it can be applied to any kind of wish. Can something this simple and accessible really work?

When I've taught WOOP to groups of teachers, health care

providers, businesspeople, or school counselors, people some-times claim that they're already performing some version of mental contrasting in their daily lives without any great results. But are they really? It's worth noting that as intuitive as mental con-trasting is, our research has shown that people seldom perform it spontaneously without knowing about the procedure and clearly intending to apply it.

In one study, A. Timur Sevincer and I triggered wishes in participants by asking the following question: "Most people value achievement and are often concerned about their profes-sional or academic accomplishments. Which personal wish about your professional or academic achievement is presently most on your mind?"[1] We analyzed the open-ended answers partici-pants gave using a rigorous content-analysis method. Only 9 percent of participants spontaneously mental contrasted, as compared with 36 percent who indulged in thoughts about the desired future, 24 percent who dwelled about their current real-ity, 11 percent who reverse contrasted, and 19 percent who per-formed some other mental process. Over a series of three studies, we found that only 16 percent of participants sponta-neously performed mental contrasting, as opposed to over 40 percent who merely imagined attaining a positive future.

This makes sense: as we've seen, indulging in positive fanta-sies is much more pleasurable than mental contrasting and it involves less mental effort. Our research suggests that to the extent people spontaneously perform mental contrasting, they tend to do so when they are feeling sad (and hence are more aware of impending problems) and when they are faced with the need to take immediate action toward a wish.[2] There are some people who are more inclined to perform mental contrasting—for instance, those who welcome mentally challenging tasks—but in general, mental contrasting is not something the vast majority of people do naturally in their daily lives. You have to *purposefully* apply WOOP to wishes that may lie dormant or situations facing you in order to reap the full benefits of mental contrasting. In fact, work we did imaging brain responses to mental contrasting showed enhanced activity in sections of the brain responsible for willfulness, memory, and more vivid, holistic thinking—a much different pattern than when people are in their normal resting state or when they are merely fantasizing about the desired future.[3]

If you do apply WOOP to your daily life, you'll find that it really does work. Over the past decade, my colleagues and I have tested the technique with individuals of different cultures, ages, and socioeconomic conditions; in men and women and with diverse wishes; in a number of settings; and both in person and online. Again and again, we've found that WOOP enables people to pursue their wishes more wisely, producing more desirable short- and long-term results than more traditional treatments or no intervention at all. If you want a proven means of regulating your energies so that you move more effectively toward fulfilling your wishes, and if you want a method that is also safe, cheap, and easy to use, you should try WOOP.

Exercising More and Eating Better

Many people today are struggling with health issues that have to do at least in part with their own behavior. In the United States, it has been estimated that "more than 75% of health care costs derive from chronic conditions" such as diabetes, heart disease, hypertension, and cancer. These conditions are influenced by lifestyle choices people make.[4] "Heart disease and stroke are the first and third leading causes of death, accounting for more than 30% of all U.S. deaths each year."[5] The problem is it's hard to change ingrained habits. So often, people try to improve their health by eating better, exercising more, or quitting cigarettes, only to find their efforts petering out after an initial period of success. For instance, about half of people who start exercising on their own give it up within six months.[6] Can WOOP help treat or prevent chronic illnesses? Can it help people better cope with and recover from debilitating injuries? Can it even help break addictions to alcohol or drugs? Our research suggests that it can.

My initial explorations in the health arena took place in the early 2000s when a large German health insurance company approached me, wondering how to better motivate people to adopt healthy behaviors.[7] Gertraud Stadler, Peter, and I collaborated with them, contacting female patients in their system ages thirty to fifty and inviting them to take part in a study on maintaining healthy lifestyles.[8] We wound up with 256 participants, whom we randomly divided into two groups: one performed WOOP and received detailed information about the importance and feasibility of regular exercise and a healthy diet, and the other merely received the information. Members of both groups were given a quiz to make sure they thoroughly understood the benefits of a healthy lifestyle.

Facilitators trained in WOOP taught the tool to members of the WOOP group over the course of one session. We asked participants to apply WOOP on their own to the wish of exercising and eating healthier whenever they could. We first let participants choose whatever kind of physical exercise they wanted to do and encouraged them to think of obstacles they personally found most daunting. We taught participants in this group how to create three types of implementation intentions. One if-then statement was designed to help them surmount the obstacle they had envisioned during mental contrasting (e.g., "If I feel I do not have time to go for a brisk walk, then I will remind myself: I will be more productive after having been outside"). Another if-then statement was designed to help participants prevent this obstacle (e.g., "If I hear the office clock chime five o'clock, then I will pack my things and leave the office to go for a run"). The third if-then statement helped participants identify a good opportunity to act (e.g., "If the sun is shining, then I will go for a thirty-minute jog in the park"). We had participants frame both long-term wishes and twenty-four-hour wishes related to exercise. Participants also applied the tool similarly in relation to their desire to eat better. Examples of WOOP applied to twenty-four-hour exercise and healthy eating wishes are given in figures 12 and 13, respectively.

WOOP Intervention

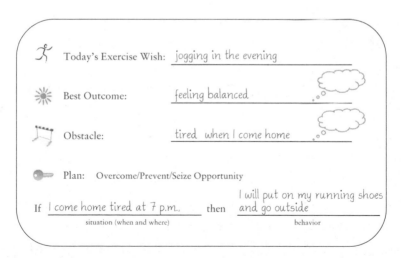

Figure 12. A WOOPed twenty-four-hour physical exercise wish with an "overcome obstacle plan."

WOOP Intervention

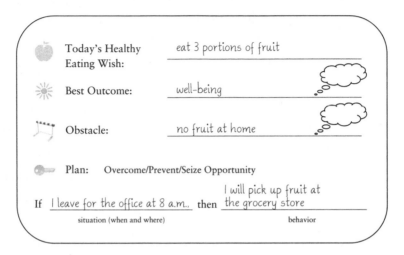

Figure 13. A WOOPed twenty-four-hour healthy eating wish with a "prevent obstacle plan."

We asked participants to create diaries logging how much they exercised and how many servings of fruit and vegetables they ate every day. To measure how they were faring in both the short and long term, we recorded their baseline numbers and checked in after one week, one month, two months, four months, and two years. The results were compelling: participants who had performed WOOP exercised *nearly twice as much* as those who had only received the basic health information, starting at one week after the intervention and continuing out to four months (see fig. 14).

Members of the WOOP group also consumed more fruit and vegetables, an effect that became more pronounced as time went on. After *two years,* members of the information-only group were eating roughly the same amount of fruit and

Exercise After Four Months

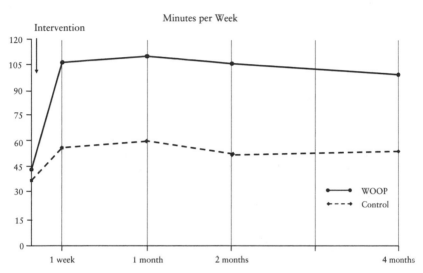

Stadler, Oettingen, & Gollwitzer (2009). *American Journal of Preventive Medicine, 36*, 29–34.

Figure 14. WOOP participants reported approximately one hour per week more physical exercise than before the intervention and as compared with the information-only control group. These differences emerged right after the intervention and were sustained until the end of the study (four months later).

vegetables as they had been before the study, while the WOOP group was up significantly—even though we did not contact participants between the four-month and two-year marks (see fig. 15).

Given that moderate physical exercise and a healthy diet are known to help people control their weight; relieve stress; lower the risks of certain types of cancers, heart disease, and type 2 diabetes; and improve quality of sleep, we concluded that WOOP could have far-reaching benefits for people's overall health.

There's one caveat, though: after two years, participants

Healthy Diet After Two Years

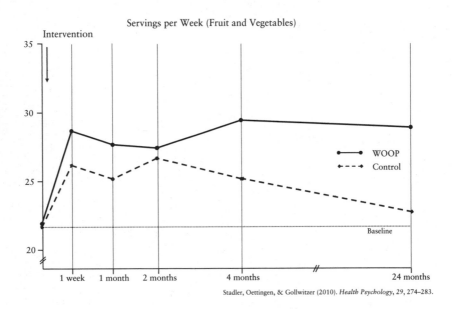

Stadler, Oettingen, & Gollwitzer (2010). *Health Psychology*, 29, 274–283.

Figure 15. WOOP participants reported eating more fruit and vegetables than before the intervention and as compared with the information-only control group. These differences emerged right after the intervention and were sustained until the end of the study (four months later). They even lasted until a follow-up assessment two years later. While WOOP participants retained their healthy eating, information-only control participants had returned to baseline.

who had performed WOOP did not differ in their exercise levels from members of the control group. Why was this? We believe that exercising is probably more difficult to change over a long period of time than diet. A single, one-hour session of WOOP will help people exercise more for a few months, but achieving a lasting benefit would require you to perform WOOP repeatedly. Other research has shown that multiple sessions allow people to sustain significant behavior change over a one-year period. Fortunately, our tool is easy to integrate into your daily life. We'll show you how to develop a powerful, lasting "WOOP habit" in the next chapter.

How WOOP Can Help People Become Healthier

To understand our results fully, it's worth considering how WOOP relates to existing health interventions. In the previous experiment, we gave our control group information about wellness because that's often what psychologists and others do in an attempt to help people live healthier lives. In the field of behavioral psychology, scholars have come up with various theories to understand how people behave in regard to their health—some of the most prominent are "protection motivation theory,"[9] "social-cognitive theory,"[10] "theory of reasoned action"[11] and the "theory of planned behavior."[12] In line with Edward C. Tolman's path-breaking experiments with rats during the early twentieth century,[13] these theories hold that in order to change people's behavior, you can do one of three things: change people's attitudes toward a behavior like diet or exercise so that they see its *value*, change the *need* or social pressure they perceive around adopting wellness behaviors, and help them gain more *knowledge* and become more confident in their ability to live healthy lives. According to these theories, modifying attitudes, social norms, and perceptions about the control people have over their behavior can lead them to set wellness goals for themselves, which in turn is linked to increased rates of physical activity.

The problem is that applying these theories often doesn't cause people to *actually change* their behavior. Take physical exercise. A study of twenty-six behavior change methods designed to target the three elements described above found that these techniques hardly caused people to exercise more.[14]

Other work has focused on changing health behaviors by altering how people think of themselves in relative terms or by making people aware of how various goals they have might conflict with one another. Some treatments for alcohol, for instance, proceed by helping people understand that two drinks a day isn't "normal," as an alcoholic might think, but is significantly above average. In this instance, the alcoholic is supposed to see himself as out of the norm and thereby become motivated to drink less.[15] Alternatively, a counselor or therapist might treat an alcoholic by helping her understand how her excessive drinking is conflicting with her goal of being a good mother or a respected professional.[16] The alcoholic's desire to achieve these other goals might spur her to cut back.

Looking beyond the health field, psychologists have also tried to change people's behavior by modifying their goals. In education, for instance, Carol S. Dweck[17] has argued that by having people believe they are susceptible to change and growth, they will come to choose learning as a goal rather than performance. This will in turn help them withstand negative feedback and not give up. A student who wants to be a good student (performance goal) will react to a setback by doubting himself; he might give up his quest because he's afraid he's no longer seen as a good student. Under Dweck's theory, a student who chooses learning as an end goal will react to the same setback with more resilience, saying "Oh, how interesting, I can use this feedback to help me learn even more in the future."

Industrial and organizational psychologists have embraced yet another approach to changing behavior. They suggest that people should focus on setting SMART goals—in other words, goals that are Specific, Measurable, Attainable, Relevant, and Time-bound. The basic idea, spelled out in Edwin Locke and Gary Latham's seminal work,[18] is that difficult and specific goals yield better performance on a given work task than easy and vague goals. If you aim to simply "do your best" on a given day, you'll accomplish far less than if you seek to complete 75 percent of your presentation, for example, or to make twenty phone calls to customers.

What's important to note about all of these approaches is that they focus on changing some part of an individual's conscious belief or goal system. With WOOP, we aren't trying to alter what people consciously think about the value of exercising, say, or about how much they exercise relative to the norm, or about how their inactivity is affecting other goals they might have. We also aren't trying to shift people's beliefs about their ability to learn and grow, nor are we trying to get them to adopt learning goals or specifically worded, challenging goals. We are instead helping people identify their wishes and mentally experience them—through a specific imagining process—so as to trigger *nonconscious effects* that enhance motivation. WOOP isn't so much an alternative to existing health behavior approaches as a complement to them. In order to be successful, WOOP depends on conscious beliefs people have that they can reasonably expect to attain their wishes. But by automating cognition, emotion, and behavior, WOOP helps people *capitalize better* on the positive attitudes and high expectations of success they may have around wishes like eating better or exercising more.

Unlike more conventional approaches, WOOP also helps people disengage from wishes that aren't practical so they are free to pursue smarter, more realistic goals. Using our method, an overweight person might disengage from a wish to run a marathon later in the year but then engage more strongly around a wish to lose twenty pounds over six months. When this happens, the person will be better positioned to stick to the more feasible wish and therefore more likely to make progress.

Additional Health Benefits

So far I've focused on how WOOP may help people prevent chronic diseases, lose weight, and eat better. Yet we have demonstrated several other ways in which WOOP can help people—healthy or sick—become healthier. If you experience chronic pain, "WOOPing" can help you recover faster by getting you to pursue more physical activity and take other measures that aid recovery. My collaborators and I invited sixty patients being treated for chronic back pain at a rehabilitation clinic to enroll in a study testing WOOP.[19] In line with their formal diagnoses, all the patients had been experiencing pain for at least six months, and their doctors had not been able to link it to a specific condition, such as a tumor or injury. The standard treatment was a three-week intensive exercise program of physical therapy, general information about pain, and education about relaxation techniques.

Half of the patients in the study were given this standard treatment and half were given the standard treatment as well as WOOP. We gave WOOP to the experimental group during two half-hour, one-on-one sessions. During the first session, participants performed mental contrasting regarding the wish of exercising more, identifying "having more fun," "enjoying more contact with other people," and "becoming more independent" as positive aspects of their desired future, with obstacles such as "The pain is too intense to move," "I'm afraid that any movement will cause damage," and "I'm afraid that if I move the pain will get worse, and I'll have to take more medication."

During the second session, participants identified how they might overcome the obstacles they had specified using different cognitive behavioral techniques. After this analysis, participants spent five minutes forming implementation intentions. For instance, one participant identified "fear of pain" as an obstacle to his goal of exercising to overcome the pain. "If I am afraid of hurting myself, then I will remember that movement is good against pain." Another said, "If it is Monday or Wednesday at five o'clock, then I will go to the fitness studio after work and exercise."

We checked in with participants after twenty-one days, when they were released from the pain program, and again at the three-month mark, measuring how capable they were physically using a series of standardized tests. Among the tests was a lifting exercise in which participants had to lift a five-kilogram box as often as they could within a two-minute time period to a series of different heights off the ground. After three weeks, patients who had performed WOOP managed thirty-five lifts on average during the two-minute period as compared with fewer than thirty for patients in the control group. After three months, members of the control group had begun to experience a decline in their physical capacity while the WOOP patients kept improving, managing nearly forty lifts, *almost double* the number of lifts as control group patients. Keep in mind this wasn't a self-reported result but an objective measure taken by professional health care providers.

We achieved similarly impressive results when we tried to enhance the amount of exercise performed by stroke patients as part of their recovery. We enrolled 201 mostly male stroke victims at a German rehabilitation center in our study.[20] One group received the standard stroke recovery treatment (health information about how to reduce stress and prevent future strokes), another group received the same treatment in a more structured and elaborate way, and a third received the more structured treatment as well as WOOP. We checked in with both groups every two and a half months up to a year after commencing the study. After a year, members of the WOOP group reported exercising for about 170 minutes every week—almost twice as much as patients who received standard treatment and over 50 minutes more than patients who received a more structured version of the standard treatment. Equally intriguing, members of the WOOP group lost an average of 4.6 kilograms (over 10 pounds) during the year, while members of both the other groups *gained* a slight amount of weight or lost only about half a kilogram. Once again, WOOP helped people recover from a debilitating condition by motivating them to overcome obstacles and take appropriate beneficial actions.

In some cases, people can become healthier not by taking constructive action but by refraining from harmful actions. Smoking cigarettes is the most important cause of preventable death, "accounting for more than 440,000 deaths, or one of every five deaths, in the United States each year."[21] Drinking too much alcohol is harmful as well, playing a role in "over 54 different diseases and injuries, including cancer of the mouth, throat, esophagus, liver, colon, and breast, liver diseases, and other cardiovascular, neurological, psychiatric, and gastrointestinal health problems."[22] Alcohol abuse among college students is rampant, leading to poor academic performance and incidences of sexual assault, among other problems.[23]

Wanting to see if we could use WOOP to reduce binge drinking, we invited seventy-two undergraduate students to participate in a study, randomly assigning them to one of two groups.[24] Students who reported being interested in drinking less filled out a questionnaire describing their alcohol usage and their drinking behavior during the previous week. After ranking how important it was to them to reduce their drinking, all students identified a behavior of theirs related to drinking that they wished to change and that was feasible to change. Students gave responses like "I would like to reduce the amount of drinks I have on a single occasion" or "I would like to never drink so much that I can't remember anything from the night before." Students also reported on the most positive outcome that would follow from drinking less (e.g., "being more productive the next day" or "I'd save tons of money"). Students then identified an obstacle standing in the way of reducing problem drinking (e.g., "classmates pressuring me" or "feeling socially inadequate") and a behavior they might adopt that would overcome the obstacle (e.g., "turn classmates down" or "be assertive").

Students in one group were led through a WOOP exercise using the elements they had already identified. Students in the other group performed a dummy exercise that was similar in structure to WOOP but that dealt with an unrelated topic: positive and negative experiences with teachers at school. A week later, we checked in with the students to gauge how much they had drunk during those seven days. Students in the WOOP group had engaged in significantly fewer bouts of drinking—an average of 1.8 during the week as compared with over 2.5 in the control group. Simply by performing a quick mental exercise, individuals who wanted to change an unhealthy behavior received a motivational boost that led to measurable results.

Think of a health-related behavior you'd like to do more or less of. Maybe it's eating healthier, smoking fewer cigarettes, spending more time outside, taking medication as prescribed by your doctor, or getting eight hours of sleep each night. Try WOOP, adapting the instructions in the last chapter to your particular health wish. Be sure that you choose a wish you have a good chance of attaining, albeit with some difficulty. You might try WOOP over the period of a few days, a week, or a month, and you might try it daily or even multiple times a day. Keep track of how often you perform the desired behavior (or don't perform the harmful behavior). If you can, keep track as well of an objective metric you can monitor—pounds lost, miles run, calories consumed, cigarettes smoked. At the end of the time period you've selected, look back at your current behavior patterns as well as the metric you've chosen. Have your habits changed in the right direction? Are you seeing meaningful progress? You might be in for a pleasant surprise.

Sustaining Better Relationships

Our research has demonstrated that WOOP works equally well for interpersonal and professional wishes. My collaborators and I investigated whether WOOP could help people lessen harmful expressions of insecurity in romantic relationships.[25] Many people experience such insecurity—doubting whether their partner feels as strongly about them as they do about their partner, and feeling anxious about particular things their partner does or says. When insecurity is present, potentially innocuous behaviors like failing to call regularly or making excuses for not going out on a date night can spiral upward into arguments and long-term conflicts, even putting the relationship in jeopardy. Cycles of insecurity take hold, as people who harbor worrisome thoughts become painfully self-conscious about their insecurity—to the point where they doubt the sincerity of any reassuring statement their partner might make.

We invited 127 students who had been in a heterosexual relationship for at least three months to participate in a study on "relationship thoughts, feelings, and behaviors." In an initial lab session, we asked students to identify an insecurity-based behavior that they thought was typical for them, that they wanted to phase out of their lives in the coming week, and that they thought they could succeed in phasing out. Participants listed behaviors like "calling too often to check where he is," "asking whom she spent time with during the day," "checking his Facebook and e-mail," or "looking through his phone log." Participants rated how often they resorted to these behaviors. We then randomly divided students into three groups. Students in one group received WOOP, students in the second performed reverse contrasting, and students in the third group were not given an exercise.

Rather than have students choose a behavioral strategy in their if-then statements, we gave them one: continue with whatever activity they had been doing before the feelings of insecurity emerged. Sample implementation intentions framed by students included "If I become untrusting, then I will continue with my ongoing activities" or "If I feel jealous, then I will continue with my ongoing activities." The point was to help students actively dismiss feelings that generated their insecure behavior so that they didn't actually partake of that behavior. We realized that students could probably generate effective strategies on their own, but by enticing them to carry on and ignore the stimulus, we were providing them with a behavioral strategy that previous research had already shown to be helpful.[26]

Each day for seven days after our initial session, we sent students an e-mail with a link to an online survey tailored to each student's specific group. WOOP students were asked to reconstruct the main elements of their WOOP exercise. Reverse contrasting students recounted the reverse contrasting elements they had generated. The "no mental exercise" students were merely asked to restate which behavior they wished to avoid or diminish. At the end of the week, we invited students back into the lab. All students reported that they had engaged in the insecurity-based behavior less than the week before, but students who had performed WOOP saw a reduction that was almost *twice as great* as that experienced by students in the other groups. Moreover, students in the WOOP group now felt more committed to their relationships than students in the other two groups.

Using WOOP at School and at Work

In other studies my colleagues and I have done, we've begun to examine the usefulness of WOOP in academic and professional contexts. The structure of these studies is similar to other research described here, but the results are well worth summarizing. In one study of high school and middle school students lead by Angela L. Duckworth, we found that WOOP helped students complete 60 percent more PSAT practice questions over their summer break than those in a control group.[27] This is a striking result, as any parent who has struggled to help their child will tell you. In a second study in Germany, parents rated middle school students who performed WOOP as having completed more homework assignments over a two-week period; significantly, this result applied to children who were at risk for ADHD and children not at risk.[28] A third study among American low-income middle school students found that those who were taught WOOP and were provided with a small WOOP reminder card (see fig. 16) saw improvements in their grade point averages and school attendance as compared with students in a control group.[29]

Given how few resources children in low-income neighborhoods have at their disposal, and how poorly many children fare as a result, these findings suggest that WOOP can serve as an important new tool children can use to improve their own odds of success.

WOOP Intervention

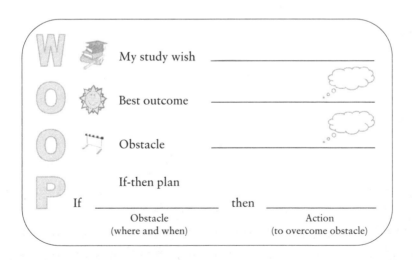

Figure 16. WOOP reminder card for students.

Another study tested whether WOOP can support adults in coping with ongoing stressors in the workplace. We demonstrated that WOOP can help health care providers in difficult professional environments reduce stress and improve their engagement with their work.[30] Three weeks into the study, providers who had performed WOOP reported significantly reduced levels of bodily and mental stress as compared with the control group. Levels of work engagement for those in the control group declined over the period while those in the WOOP group reported being *more* engaged.

The Promise of WOOP

My colleagues and I are continuing to research the effectiveness of WOOP in many different contexts and with different kinds of wishes. As of this writing, we are studying WOOP's effectiveness among marathon runners, members of a semiprofessional rowing team, people struggling with making complex decisions, people who feel lonely and anxious, and people facing an imminent life change, among others. Since WOOP is content neutral, it is applicable to virtually anything in life, from team collaboration to parenting, spending habits to studying, choosing a career to choosing what to have for breakfast. The more areas we explore in our studies, the more complete our understanding will be of the applicability and benefits of WOOP. But our preliminary conclusions after a decade of research are already clear. As a tool for regulating our energies and efforts, WOOP holds great potential working for people in various kinds of life circumstances, whether you're rich or poor, a student or a working professional, a European or an American.

So many popular self-help programs and strategies aren't

scientifically validated. If you have something in your life that you'd really like to change—or even if you just want to enjoy it even more—you'd be well advised to dispense with the trendy "positive thinking" approach and give WOOP a try. You also might think about the wider social implications of this method. Recognizing the difficulty individuals have in organizing their lives, we so often turn to government and policy making to get people to behave more constructively. Through laws and regulations, we try to get people to do things like eat better, stay off drugs, work harder, and take better care of their families. While WOOP can hardly substitute for social regulation, it can serve as an important complementary tool, enabling individuals to better regulate their own lives for the betterment of all.

WOOP is by no means a cure-all, but think of how much in our imperfect world might be changed if millions of people were practicing WOOP on a regular basis. How much might we save in lives and financial resources if we were able to get millions of people to eat healthier, exercise more, or cut down on cigarette smoking? How many marriages might be saved if we could get millions of partners to interact in more reasonable, less anxious ways? How much more productive might our economy be if millions of employees were less stressed-out and more engaged at work? How much better might our society function if our children were able to study better and pursue more energetically the career paths that were right for them?

We've only begun to find out.

Chapter Eight

. . . .

Your Friend for Life

This book has taken you inside the new science of motivation, leading you through a broad and deep rethinking of positive thinking. We have examined the limitations of conventional positive thinking, explained why positive thinking doesn't work as well as many people believe, introduced the alternate strategy of mental contrasting, described why it works using research in the confines of the lab, explored how we developed mental contrasting into the practical tool called WOOP, and shown how people have successfully used WOOP to solve pressing problems or help their wishes come true. I'd now like to explore the *experience* of using WOOP and provide you with a series of guidelines for using this tool effectively in your own life. I base these guidelines not just on the studies recounted in this book but also on the experiences I've had teaching WOOP to people in many contexts on two continents.

Scientific studies that confirm the power of WOOP might lead you to believe that WOOP is an easy fix, a "pill" you swallow to feel an immediate result. Participants in our studies show important, long-term changes in their behavior—such as eating more vegetables, exercising more, drinking less—after as little as a single WOOP session. Yet WOOP is more than a one-off way of dealing with a particular concern or wish. It's a *living tool* that you can use in your everyday life. Practiced daily over an extended period of time, WOOP enables you to not only solve specific problems or wishes, but live a life that is balanced, meaningful, and generally happy.

I like to think of WOOP as similar to a guide dog leading the blind. You and I are the blind. We go about our daily lives not quite understanding who we really are, what we really want, or what stands in our way. When we don't get what we think we want right away, we tend to make excuses, which only leads us farther astray. We get stuck, banging our heads against obstacles over and over again without making any progress. We also get caught up in our perception of our wishes, locking ourselves into obsessive thoughts—what in French are called idées fixes. We think, "I *have* to do X" or "I need to finish Y before I can tackle Z" or "It's not proper for me to do W."

Then along comes WOOP, our furry little friend. WOOP isn't emotionally or ideologically invested in W, X, Y, or Z. WOOP isn't invested in any particular solution or outcome. It's a process for helping you find your path. If you take time to familiarize yourself with WOOP, if you "feed" it with ideas and give it your attention, you can consistently rely on it to show you the way and help you make decisions. Instead of feeling your way step-by-halting-step, you can behave more securely. You feel less alone, because you have a resource at your side that goes wherever you do. When you do go astray in your thinking or actions, WOOP is always there to put you back on track. The result is steady progress, growth, and engagement with the world. Just as a Seeing Eye dog gives the blind an ability to get out and live life to the fullest, so does WOOP. It is your trusty companion through life, whether you're eight or eighty-eight.

As you increasingly integrate WOOP into your life, you'll find that you get better at it and use it to adapt to your changing needs, challenges, and life circumstances. The specific wishes you WOOPed at the beginning may come true, but they may not—and that's fine. Over the course of successive WOOP sessions, as you gain insight into hidden obstacles in your path, you may discover that your initial desires were unrealistic or not as fulfilling as you originally thought, or that they conflicted with other desires you have. New desires or goals may emerge that you hadn't considered before and that seem more alluring. Certain parts of your initial wishes may pop out at you, and others will seem to fall away because they pose greater challenges and offer fewer rewards. You may focus your WOOP sessions not primarily on significant wishes, but on smaller challenges you face in your daily life. You may discover that your wishes are good and that the obstacles are surmountable, but that the timing isn't right or that you haven't been using the right tools to overcome your obstacles.

Certainly you will achieve a better understanding of your wishes and concerns and the facets of your life that impede them. Obsessive ideas will fall away and a journey of exploration will commence, one that affects multiple dimensions of your life all at once. You will pursue *real* wishes, ones that resonate with you and that are feasible. You'll feel more committed, connected, calm, and contented. And you'll be more excited to see what is yet to come. That's what the science implies. And it's what my own personal experience with WOOP bears out.

Begin at the Beginning

You already know the basic WOOP technique—so how do you deploy it? Begin at the beginning, wherever that happens to be for you. Many people I meet find it helpful to begin WOOP by practicing first in connection with a deep-seated wish that has been lying dormant or has been pushed aside in their consciousness. We all have subtler, more complex wishes that we feel passionate about but that we don't dare contemplate. Maybe we yearn for a career change but avoid that wish because we're afraid to quit our job. Maybe we feel wounded by a relationship that ruptured long ago, but we don't want to admit to ourselves that we want to renew the relationship or bring it to proper closure. By using WOOP to better understand these more intense wishes, people get a visceral experience of what WOOP is and how it works. From there, they are in a position to apply WOOP to more mundane wishes, such as how to proceed with an unpleasant conversation or how to make the most of a free afternoon.

Often it takes a WOOP exercise itself to unearth emotional

wishes lying just below the surface. An alcoholic trying WOOP for the first time might initially frame her wish by saying, "How nice it would be not to drink anymore." The alcoholic's natural response might be "Well, yeah, it would be nice not to drink, but it would also be nice to drink!" In other words, it can be tough for an alcoholic to generate positive fantasies about *not* drinking.

Stopping here and asking, "What do I *really* wish for at this particular moment in time?" might cause the alcoholic to reply, "a better relationship with my wife" or "to be a contributing member of my work team again" or "to be a better parent." Now, these are emotionally powerful wishes. The obstacle to any of these wishes might well turn out to be drinking, in which case the alcoholic can do another WOOP, more fully aware of how much the wish of no longer drinking matters to him.

In addition to starting with a more substantial or emotional wish, also begin by trying to WOOP a short, twenty-four-hour wish. You might say, "In the next twenty-four hours, I would really like to have a nice dinner with my spouse" or "In the next twenty-four hours, I would like to finish the project I'm working on." What would be the best outcome if your wish came true? Hold this outcome in your mind and imagine it. What holds you back from achieving your wish? Identify your main internal obstacle, again holding it in your mind and imagining it. Finally, think of how you might overcome the obstacle, creating an "if *obstacle*, then *action to overcome*" plan for yourself. Repeat this plan once to yourself to fix it in your mind. You can perform WOOP in your mind or write it down on a WOOP reminder card (see fig. 17).

WOOP Four-Step Technique

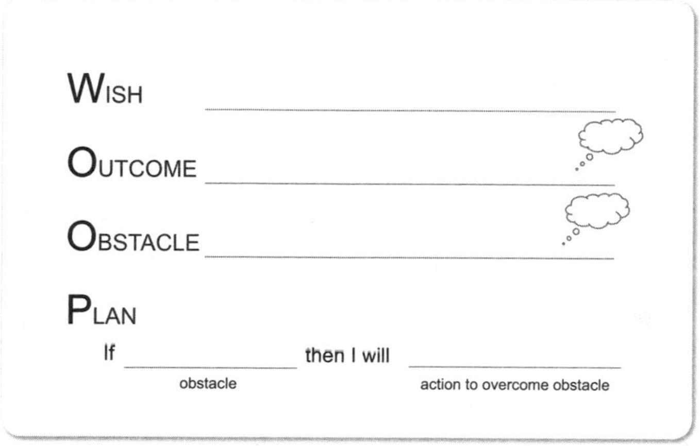

WISH _____

OUTCOME _____

OBSTACLE _____

PLAN

If _____ then I will _____
       obstacle   action to overcome obstacle

Figure 17. WOOP reminder card for daily use.

Develop YOUR Daily Practice

Once you've tried WOOP a couple of times and feel comfortable with it, continue to experiment. Try using WOOP with different kinds of wishes, at different times of day, in different contexts or situations. Develop a "WOOP habit." Many people I know like to do WOOP first thing in the morning or as they're falling asleep at night. Others make a point of doing one every day during their morning commute. A writer I know began doing WOOP at the beginning of each writing session, to stay razor focused and to get a better handle on feelings that were impeding his work. If you're a corporate manager, try doing WOOP when you first come into work each morning or when you're wrapping up for the day. If you're anxious about public speaking, perform WOOP before every speech you make. Because WOOP is content neutral, the possibilities are endless. And the more you do WOOP in one context, the more you'll unexpectedly see its effects popping up elsewhere in your life.

If you're new to WOOP, be sure to try it in the morning. I do so and find that it serves as a great way of preparing for the day. In the evening, I'll remember my morning's WOOP and observe how the day went; often, I'll find that my behavior was very much guided by my WOOPed wishes and the steps I identified to prevent or overcome obstacles, without intending or realizing it. You'll really understand the power of WOOP as a way of programming yourself cognitively; you'll feel as if an invisible hand guided you during the day. Your nonconscious mind was at work, allowing for change that feels effortless. Further, you'll find that you're easily developing new habits, even though habits are supposed to require considerable practice in order to take root.[1]

Whatever you do to experiment, be sure to stay true to the basic format of the exercise. Carve out some mental space for yourself, resisting the urge to text or check e-mail and gaining as much solitude as you can. Then take yourself through the four steps without interruption. Try to catch yourself if your mind starts to wander between steps. Don't reverse the order or leave out a step, and try to be as specific as you can in formulating your wishes, outcomes, and obstacles. In line with the discussion in chapter 6, really take time to imagine your desired future as well as what stands in the way. Let the images flow!

If you want to take action toward a desired future, then be sure to choose wishes that are challenging but still attainable for you. WOOP won't help you live more fully if your wish is to live on planet Neptune or become a billionaire within a year.

Even here, though, you need to experiment and feel out the WOOP procedure as you go. Sometimes we think that our wishes are within reach only to find during WOOP that the obstacles are bigger than we anticipated; in these cases, WOOP frees us to disengage from the wish and go on to other, more practicable wishes. Other times, wishes that at first glance seem beyond our control turn out to be very or at least partially manageable. Often, the big discovery here is that we have more internal resources at our disposal than we ever imagined.

Wishes framed around the desire to overcome pain from a physical condition are a case in point. Many people wouldn't think of treating pain with a visualization technique; there are pills for that, right? Yet we saw that back pain sufferers recovered better with WOOP because they were inclined to move and exercise more. Likewise, a friend of mine had a painful sinus condition and performed WOOP with the wish "that my headaches go away." They didn't go away entirely but they did lessen somewhat. The obstacle that emerged during the exercise was "I become stressed out and worried by my headaches." As my friend discovered, the feeling of being stressed and worried was not causing the headaches, but it *was* making them more painful. By addressing the feeling, she could reduce her suffering.

Take WOOP Mobile

To facilitate your daily practice, we have created free smartphone apps[2] that lead you through the four steps and allow you to track your wishes over time and see how far they've gotten to completion (see woopmylife.org). We first designed an app[3] for schoolchildren in low-income neighborhoods—in particular, high school students—to help them achieve their wish of attending college (the "wooptoandthroughcollege" app). Many adolescents have a hard time reaching goals that require sustained self-discipline; low-income teens who wish to attend college are especially vulnerable, since they often aren't familiar with the steps required to attend college and don't have access to SAT coaches, peer support groups, and other sources of help.[4] Given the evidence-based success of WOOP as a behavior change tool, we thought an app would be a fun, intuitive way to expose children and adolescents to the exercise. By allowing them to share their wishes and the status of their wishes with others on Facebook, the app helps them connect with a community and exchange their problems and concerns as well as the strategies to solve them.

More recently, we have released a version of an app specifically designed for use by adults in their professional and personal lives. By prompting you to run through each of the four steps, the app can help you avoid the most common traps people fall into when doing WOOP. You feel like you're guided through the exercise by a trusty friend—especially useful when you're tired and don't want to focus on getting WOOP right. Since you're typing your wishes, outcomes, obstacles, and plans into the app, you're forced to be very specific in framing your responses. You're also explicitly encouraged to take the time to virtually experience your future and self-identified obstacle in your mind.

Even if you're experienced with WOOP, the app is useful as a means of keeping yourself focused on the right way to complete the exercise. Because the app lets you log your WOOPs, categorizing them as either personal or professional, and as short term or long term, you can use it to see how your wishes have changed over time, how your naming and framing of the obstacles have changed, and how you may have returned repeatedly to the same wish. It can serve you as a kind of diary of your desires, giving you a window into your progress over time. The app also helps you integrate WOOP into your daily routines. People who try WOOP sometimes shrink from using the exercise as often as they could; they believe they need to find a perfect time and place to be alone with one's thoughts and it all seems daunting. With the app in their pockets, people feel encouraged to WOOP whenever or wherever they happen to be.

Although the prerequisite for doing WOOP is creating a mental space, you don't need absolute quiet or privacy. Having the app handy and seeing it on the screen of your phone reminds you to carve out precious moments for yourself to do WOOP while sitting in the airport, while you're stuck in a traffic jam, or while you're waiting your turn at the dentist. This way, you are better able to do WOOP in the heat of everyday life, applying it to pressing tasks as they present themselves. You wind up doing fewer silly things, such as trying to work when you're tired or procrastinating when you're faced with a difficult task. You're not just focused in a general way—but hour to hour and minute to minute.

Fine-Tune Your Wishes

One of the reasons it's important to work with WOOP daily is that you need sufficient opportunity to fine-tune your wishes to changing conditions and outcomes. A salesperson might adopt an initial wish of making ten sales a day. The best outcome of that wish would be "I will feel satisfied that I worked hard and at the end of the day, I can go to my boss and feel confident in my job performance." What stands in the way might be "I don't have time to make enough sales calls." Why don't you have enough time? "Because I am spending more time than I should chatting with colleagues." The if-then plan may become "If I find myself chatting with a colleague, then I'll politely excuse myself and go back to the phone to make more sales calls." Let's say you put this if-then plan into practice, and you're partially successful: you've done five sales instead of your usual three or four. Instead of getting discouraged and thinking WOOP didn't work, you can ask yourself whether ten calls a day was realistic to begin with. Maybe the next day you'll reframe your wish, shooting for six sales calls a day. And maybe by late the next morning, when you've had a run of success and already notched four of the six wished-for sales, you do another WOOP to cover the afternoon. "During the afternoon, I want to call enough prospective customers so I can get seven sales for today." Give yourself a chance to adjust your wishes to match what you discover you're able to accomplish. In this way, you stay flexible and bring yourself closer to your goal while not getting frustrated if things don't go exactly as planned.

Sometimes it isn't a question of adjusting the magnitude of a wish as it is of letting new, deeper wishes unfold. Ray, a man who is overweight and out of shape, might frame his wish as losing twenty pounds in six months. Doing WOOP, Ray realizes that the obstacle standing in his way is an issue such as binge eating. But what is the *inner* obstacle that causes him to binge eat? He might discover that he binge eats because he "feels alone" or "leads a life that isn't that fulfilling," and that he fills the emotional void by eating. What can he do to lead a less lonely life? "Well," Ray says, "I love to surf, and I could meet people that way." His if-then plan becomes "The next time I feel alone, I will go online and find a surfing club to join."

Ray might also discover that feeling less alone or becoming more connected could be his next wish. Using WOOP for this wish, he finds that the critical obstacle standing in the way are his feelings of inadequacy due to instances in his past when people called him socially awkward. He thinks of overcoming this obstacle by calling a supportive friend. But this only leads to another in this series of cascading wishes as Ray realizes how hard it is to find time in his busy schedule to actually call people and talk to them on the phone. What stands in the way? He wastes so much time on the Internet each evening that he has little room for other pursuits. The solution pops into Ray's mind: turn off the computer right now, call the friend, and plan a dinner for the following evening. Off Ray goes toward fulfilling his last wish, which in turn will ultimately lead him to fulfill his original goal of losing twenty pounds.

As this example suggests, fine-tuning our wishes can entail refining our understanding of the internal obstacles we face. There is no single, "correct" obstacle in our paths. We determine that an obstacle is "correct" by taking ourselves through honest examination of answers we might give to the question "What is holding me back?" If we initially come up with an answer like "I don't have enough time," it's important to ask, "*Why* don't I have enough time?" Often there is an underlying, internal obstacle—maybe it's a fear we feel that causes us to waste time by procrastinating. Or maybe we feel insecure in our relationships and we don't have enough time because we spend too much time socializing when we don't even want to be doing that. We can stay at a superficial level with our WOOP exercises—or we can choose to go deeper. We can let the plunge into our deeper obstacles take place gradually as we come at our wishes and concerns again and again.

When I first led my colleague Barbara through WOOP, she told me that her wish was to get stronger in French by studying vocabulary for an hour in the evening. The obstacle she identified was her "tendency to plan to study on a given day but then not to drive forward with the plan." When I asked her why she tended to abandon her plan to study, she said that she got distracted by other things going on around her. Okay, but why? I asked. Here Barbara was stumped. She didn't know exactly why. "It's got something to do with my relationship with my partner; I refuse to stand my ground when I have something I want. I let him dictate my evenings, actually my whole schedule, and then become distracted with other tasks." She faced a choice: she could continue with the WOOP exercise and come up with a plan for what to do when she found herself getting distracted, or she could probe to the deepest obstacle undercutting her ability to be assertive with her partner and do an if-then plan around that. If Barbara did this extra work, she would likely address multiple issues in her life simultaneously and come up with integrative solutions that would help her move ahead on multiple fronts at once. Barbara decided she wasn't emotionally ready for that, so for now she formed an if-then plan that would help her in the moment when she found herself caving on her studying: "If I find myself getting distracted from studying vocabulary, then I will explain to my partner that I feel strongly about studying French and need the hour in the evening."

The more you put into your WOOP practice, the more you get out of it. If you are inclined to go as deep as possible in identifying the obstacle, then be honest with yourself. What really *does* stand in your way? You don't need to tell anyone the real answer—just tell yourself. The obstacle might not be flattering. It might entail a hit to your ego. It might be a truth about yourself that you've long avoided facing. That's fine. Now is the time to look at it. Announce it to yourself as part of the WOOP exercise. You'll find that by understanding what *truly* holds you back, clear actions you can take to overcome the obstacle will naturally unfold. WOOP challenges us to get rid of all the excuses we normally tell ourselves—to stop blaming other people or external conditions and focus all our attention on what it is in us that keeps us from moving forward. With the excuses gone, the path to our dreams opens up before us.

Be Patient

Some people start using WOOP not to achieve more clarity but to promptly fulfill a specific dream. They may become disappointed if it doesn't work right away and give up after the first try. If you performed WOOP and have not seen the immediate results you expected, there are many possible reasons. Perhaps you aren't following the procedure correctly or perhaps the wish you chose was too ambitious and you need to fine-tune it. Whatever the case, try not to become discouraged and rush to the conclusion that WOOP won't work. Instead, make some adjustments and try it again. When it comes to framing our wishes, one of WOOP's great benefits is precisely that it helps you select and pursue wishes that are feasible for you and to let go of wishes that are not.

For instance, my colleague Linda did WOOP in the afternoon and chose as her wish getting up at 6 a.m. the next morning to catch up on her huge pile of unanswered e-mails. When she went to bed at 12:30 a.m., after attending a work dinner, she decided that she was certainly *not* going to get up at 6 a.m. but instead sleep in so that she could feel rested for the entire day. The next day when I saw her, she complained that WOOP had not worked for her in the slightest. I explained that in fact WOOP had worked, because it had caused her to decisively choose an alternative, more beneficial path. In her WOOP, she had opted for an unrealistic wish. The obstacle in her path—the need to attend a late-night work dinner—had been simply too large to surmount, and she had understandably abandoned her wish for a better alternative path. Going forward, she might try choosing a slightly different goal of catching up on e-mails only after nights when she can expect to sleep for eight hours.

Sometimes when people tell me that WOOP hasn't worked for them, I find they have not disengaged from their wishes like Linda did but have accomplished their wishes without realizing it. For example, Claire used WOOP to finally tackle her wish of eating less red meat. Three weeks later, when I asked how much meat she has consumed, she replied, "Well with the meat, I'm fine, I didn't eat any this past week, but I still had my usual glass of wine with dinner, so WOOP hasn't really worked; I did not change my diet that much." In this instance, Claire was writing off her accomplishment of eating less red meat as negligible, focusing only on a newer wish that she hadn't yet attained—and that she hadn't even WOOPed. Don't be so quick to dismiss what you've accomplished through WOOP. We're so used to the notion that accomplishment requires a serious expenditure of effort. WOOP, as we've seen, works by acting on our nonconscious minds. As a result, individuals will often make substantial progress toward their wishes without even being aware of it. They might even feel that they've failed when in fact objective measurements suggest otherwise. Be sure to track wishes as you've achieved them.

When people start to keep track of wishes, they sometimes find it shocking just how much WOOP has changed their lives over time. One attorney I know was about to be appointed chairman of his firm. He knew he had a tendency to behave in an autocratic way and he wanted to change that and become "nicer." He wanted to listen to people's concerns and become more empathetic. During his summer vacation he WOOPed that wish and then forgot all about it. By December of that year, when he had been chairman for over three months, he happened to come across his original written WOOP in a desk drawer. He was pleased to notice that during the preceding months he *was* behaving nicely and empathetically toward his colleagues. Working on his nonconscious mind, WOOP had nudged him imperceptibly in the direction of his goal.

When evaluating your progress with WOOP, be sure to take into account your life as a whole. WOOP leads people to what psychologists call "integrative solutions"—solutions that span and involve multiple areas. Gil turned to WOOP because he wanted to sleep better. For years, his anxiety caused him to wake up once or twice a night and he had trouble falling back asleep. A month after performing a nightly WOOP around the wish of getting a restful night's sleep, he found that he was regularly sleeping seven to eight hours without waking up. But he noticed something else: he was making progress in his workouts, substantially upping the time he spent exercising, and he was more focused and effective in his work than he had been in a long time.

Of course, we cannot definitively attribute all of this to WOOP. Perhaps by sleeping better, Gil was able to do other things better. Perhaps by confronting the underlying internal obstacle that was impeding his sleeping, Gil was also able to take on the same obstacle in other areas and improve his exercise and work performance. The cognitive and behavioral changes triggered by WOOP might have interacted with other things Gil consciously or unconsciously did to address his sleep problem, in ways that were impossible for him to unravel. The energy leashed by the WOOP exercise itself might have played a role. WOOP has been shown to bring about changes in groups of people, but individuals applying WOOP should evaluate it by paying close attention to the specific and unique changes they might notice in their own lives.

Use WOOP in Stressful Situations

Another instance in which WOOP can prove helpful is dealing with situations of acute or continued stress: a business presentation you're about to make, a flight you need to take, a boss who intimidates you but whom you have to work with. Casual users of WOOP will often not think to apply the tool in stressful times; they're too busy reacting to the stressor. If you have developed a daily WOOP practice, however, you are more inclined to stop yourself in the heat of the moment and say, "Hold on. Use WOOP!"

Let's say you're about to go onstage to make a presentation in front of 200 people. You take three minutes out to do your WOOP. Your wish? To do a good job on the presentation. Your outcome? That you get your message across, and that you feel in synch with your audience. Imagine the outcome; experience it in your mind. What is it *in you* that stands in the way? Maybe it is a general anxiety that "I will embarrass myself," or a specific technical obstacle such as "I speak too fast" or "I tend to forget the key points." From there the plans materialize easily. "If I feel anxious, then I'll remind myself that I've succeeded with presentations in the past." "If I find myself speaking too fast, I'll slow down." "If I find that I've forgotten a key point, I will make a mental note to weave it in at the end of the presentation." With such a plan in place, and the cognitive connections between future, obstacle, and helpful behaviors forged in your nonconscious mind, you are now positioned to handle your obstacle and move ahead confidently in the stressful situation.

In the business world, stressful times often emerge because we're tasked with doing so many things at the same time. WOOP can help you overcome hidden obstacles and do what you must to satisfy your competing priorities. In studies described earlier in the book, my collaborators and I used mental contrasting and WOOP to help health care providers manage their time better so that they prevented demands from piling up and causing stress. To understand how this might work, imagine you're sitting in a business meeting at 5 p.m., and you know that in fifteen minutes your four-year-old will be standing outside his nursery school in the cold if you don't stop the meeting and leave to pick him up. Doing WOOP with the wish of getting out of the meeting in time, you discover that your *real* obstacle is timidity, not feeling confident enough to speak up at the right time and say to colleagues and bosses, "Look, in five minutes, I really have to go." With that understanding in place, you're led naturally to a solution: finding a friendly and effective way to say good-bye instead of unsuccessfully trying for ten minutes to wheedle your way out of the meeting and then rushing to pick up your child and arriving stressed out and frazzled. In one application of WOOP, you've found a way to handle a stressful situation that likely recurs multiple times in a single week. Think of how your life might change for the better.

Oftentimes, we face stressful external situations that we can't change or overcome—a boss who hates us and berates us in public, for instance. Even if we can't do anything about the boss, WOOP can still help us to cope with him in a way that leaves us happy and with our self-respect intact. Wishing to cope with a legitimate and unavoidable external challenge, we ask ourselves what obstacle inside us might be preventing us from coping as effectively as possible. Maybe what stands in our way is our tendency to feel victimized or to dwell on feelings of disgruntlement or our fear of speaking up and making our feelings known. We can't change the world in these most difficult of situations, but we can reclaim a sense of empowerment by discovering how *we* wish to respond and then using WOOP to actually respond in those ways.

Use WOOP to Combat Persistent Anxiety

What if you're not feeling stressed but rather irrationally anxious about something you will face in the future? In chapter 4, I presented a study in which we used mental contrasting to help people confront fears, specifically fears that adolescents had about peers in other ethnic groups. If you feel unjustifiably anxious about your upcoming tax return (knowing that in reality you have sufficient funds to pay your taxes), try addressing it by adapting WOOP. Instead of first defining a wish and fantasizing about a positive future, identify the worst possible outcome that could arise when you receive this year's tax return. Vividly elaborate this worst outcome in your mind. Think of all the money you're afraid you'll owe and how hard of a time you'll have paying your tax bill. Then, identify and imagine the positive present reality that stands in the way of the negative future coming to pass. In this case, you might imagine the fact that you currently have sufficient funds in your bank account to pay your likely tax bill or the fact that you anticipate getting a bonus check at Christmas that will help with your taxes. Finally, create an if-then plan for yourself: "If I start to worry about my taxes, then I will remind myself that I have enough in my bank account to cover it."

So often we become locked in to threatening ideas and don't allow ourselves to mentally experience alternative possibilities or options. Often, taking the time to let our minds wander and then focus on the reassuring present reality can set us free from obsessive thoughts. And the if-then plan gives us a strategy to fall back on whenever our habitual fears recur. If you're afraid of failing as a graduate student, remind yourself of all the success you've had and peer support you are currently receiving. If you're irrationally afraid of losing your job, remind yourself of the reassuring conversation your boss just had with you. Don't give in to your fear. Try WOOPing it. You'll feel calmer, less helpless, and more in control. The fear washes out of you and you feel liberated in the moment. If you're plagued by unjustified anxiety, a small victory like this can give you confidence that when anxiety arises again, you can handle it.

Find Clarity

Beyond helping us take action (or refrain from action) more effectively and containing our fears, WOOP can serve us by helping us gain more clarity. Sometimes we don't have a clear wish but instead simply want to resolve a question or decision we face. "Shall I travel across the country to see an old friend, or not?" "Shall I spend the evening talking with my daughter, or not?" Framing a possible course of action as a wish and then imagining the obstacles can help us resolve such dilemmas. In effect, we're not using WOOP but merely the mental contrasting portion of it. In the case of the cross-country trip, taking the trip becomes our wish. The outcome: "It would be so much fun to see my friend and I'd feel rooted and connected." So what's the obstacle? "Well, money. If I spend money on a plane ticket, I won't be able to afford a new car. And I *really* need a new car—that has to be my top priority." Okay, the answer is clear: "I shouldn't take that cross-country trip." Such clarity in turn clears the way for more decisive action—in this case, purchase of the car.

Maybe what you're unclear about isn't a specific decision point but simply a vague, unsettling feeling you have. "Why do I dread seeing my high school friend Garry this weekend?" In such situations, you can frame as a wish the overcoming of your uneasiness. "Wouldn't it be nice to get through the coming weekend and have a great time with Garry?"

You then proceed to outline the outcome. Maybe it's something like "feeling whole" or "feeling relaxed" or "bonding with Garry this weekend." The next step of WOOP poses the vital question: What is it *in you* that stands in the way? You're forced for the first time to really identify and *think* about the obstacle that underlies your vague feelings toward seeing Garry. And when you do that, you start to gain valuable new insight into the situation. "I dread seeing Garry because he always says something that makes me feel insecure, and I'm afraid he'll do the same thing again." Pondering this in turn can lead to an even deeper insight: "I feel insecure when I'm in Garry's presence because he is successful at his job and I've always felt second-rate compared to him, even though I know I'm doing well for myself." From here you can take it even further, or you can make an if-then plan that allows you to enjoy your time with Garry. "If I start to feel insecure when I'm with Garry, then I'll remind myself of all I have accomplished in my life." However your time with Garry goes, you have come to understand feelings of yours that had been lingering under the surface. You've solved a mystery for yourself and in some small (or perhaps large) way, enriched your life. Who knows—perhaps your tendency to compare yourself unfavorably with Garry or others impedes other wishes you have as well.

Start WOOP at a Young Age

A number of studies described in this book indicate that mental contrasting and WOOP help children regulate their efforts to achieve wishes better. In some respects, children have a huge advantage over adults in learning and working with this tool. Many adults are resistant to putting their rational thought aside and giving themselves over to the free flow of imagery. They have a hard time putting their egos aside and naming internal obstacles to their wishes. They often are less in touch with their wishes than children and feel shyer about articulating them.

In our studies, we have worked with children as young as seven or eight. We performed written WOOP exercises with these children since they were able to write, but there is no reason WOOP can't work with even younger children when administered orally. With children, we usually find WOOP helpful in terms of regulating emotions that threaten to spiral out of control and affect school performance. One third grader at a low-income school would cry for hours at any small frustration that would emerge during the school day. This went on for years and nothing the teachers or counselors tried improved the situation. One day, the school principal led him through WOOP using the smartphone app. The if-then plan had the child taking five deep breaths if he became frustrated. A few days later, the child began to have a breakdown and begged his teacher for the principal's phone. The teacher had no idea what the child was talking about. Why in the world would he want the principal's phone? "I need the phone to do WOOP so I won't break down," the child said with tears in his eyes. Familiar with WOOP, the teacher instructed the child to do the exercise in his head. The child did so and was able to calm down.[5]

When beginning to perform WOOP with a child, make sure to find a wish that the child (and not you) feels passionate about. *You* might want the wish to be "Wouldn't it be great to get your homework done?" But getting homework done might not strike your child as his or her greatest wish. I asked one little girl what her dearest wish was and she said, "I want to be a dancer!" I asked her the outcome and we then proceeded on to the obstacle. "The obstacle," she said, "is I won't finish school, so I won't be able to become a dancer." I went on to do some of the same probing of the obstacle that we do with adults. "What will prevent you from finishing school?"

"I'm not good enough at schoolwork."

"Why aren't you good enough?"

"Because I don't get good grades in English or math."

"Why don't you?"

"Because I don't do my homework."

"Why don't you do your homework?"

"Because I watch TV in the afternoon."

We now had the obstacle—too much television watching in the afternoon. Now it was a simple matter to come up with an if-then plan. "If I start watching TV in the afternoon, then I will switch it off and do my homework instead." If we had started with "doing more homework" as the wish, the child wouldn't have become engaged in the exercise. By starting with a wish that the child felt really passionate about (and around which she was able to create positive fantasies), she was able to perceive television watching in a new light—as a serious impediment to her dreams.

One reason I recommend using WOOP with children is that the benefits of WOOP only increase the earlier you begin using it. In recent decades, some educational and parenting experts have shrunk away from enforcing boundaries (e.g., curfews), manners (e.g., keeping your voice down in a restaurant), and everyday rituals (e.g., formal dinner times), not wishing to restrict children's freedom to explore. Though this approach has its advantages, one disadvantage is that children sometimes aren't learning some of the skills and habits they need to regulate their energies and achieve their goals. WOOP gives children strategies they can use to perform better. If you start children on WOOP at a young age, they will begin moving toward their dreams sooner. They will be better able to adopt basic behaviors required in order to get along in the world, such as listening to others, learning from feedback, or controlling emotions. Once these behaviors are in place, they become habits on which children can build.

Toward Freedom

WOOP is like any tool—a hammer, a piano, a bicycle—in that people will use it in different ways and to different ends. In some situations, people will use WOOP to adjust their wishes, whereas in other circumstances they will use it to identify obstacles that prove difficult to overcome, to disengage from pursuits that are making them unhappy, to pursue dreams that have eluded them in the past, or simply to understand their wishes better. No matter how you choose to use WOOP, remember that this strategy is fundamentally about connecting to others and to the world at large. Yes, you learn a lot about yourself through the process of mental contrasting, but that self-knowledge always exists in service to the larger purpose of a connection with others and the world.

People today are always in motion, running toward and away from wishes and goals—toward and away from connections. WOOP allows you to tap into this constant movement, to join it, to become part of the flow of life, to move in a particular direction. Using WOOP to overcome fears and anxieties allows you to welcome the outside in; you free yourself to connect with others. Even in the case of wishes that seem on the surface to only involve you—a fitness or health wish for example, such as sleeping better, weighing less, or eating better—using WOOP enables you to engage more actively with life. You feel better and you have more energy, so you're more inclined to participate in activities you might have shied away from before. Even the act of engaging in WOOP tends to get you outside of yourself by prompting you to identify the obstacle, which very often involves someone else (consider Barbara's case, for instance, in which the obstacle to studying French in the evening turned out to be a relationship dynamic involving her partner).

WOOP is an opportunity to get unstuck and come out of your shell. Even in societies in which certain freedoms are guaranteed and our choices of action are many, we all don't necessarily have the ability to be free, because we suffer from hang-ups or sensitivities that bedevil us. We tell ourselves we can't do certain things. We fail to look our insecurities in the face, blaming others or circumstances outside of us for our frustrations. We need to work at becoming free. We need to regulate ourselves so that at each moment we pursue what we actually *want* to pursue, not necessarily what other people tell us to pursue or what we think they want us to pursue. We also have to regulate ourselves so that we can wisely choose among the thousands of paths open to us. Something as simple as taking a moment to envision a longed-for future and then identifying how we are blocking our own wishes makes all the difference. Cutting through layers of excuses and untested beliefs, sifting through conflicting priorities, we launch ourselves toward our feasible dreams and away from unfeasible ones. Mobilizing our nonconscious minds, we lock in to our attainable desires and ensure that we're moving ahead along our chosen paths with our full energies.

We are just beginning to rethink positive thinking, evolving the new science of motivation and mobilizing it to improve individuals' lives and address social problems. But what we do know is very clear. To make the most of our lives, we must face up to the role we play in hamstringing our own wishes. Doing so isn't complicated, but it is profound and life changing. With WOOP and mental contrasting, we motivate and empower ourselves to take action when it will really benefit us and those around us. We unleash powerful forces within us so that we can change habits of thought and behavior we've had for years. It sounds like magic, and it feels like magic, but the science shows it's real. Wishing you good luck on your journey of discovery, I'll end with two vital questions that I hope you never stop asking yourself: What is your dearest wish? What holds you back from achieving it?

Acknowledgments

What is my wish? That I could sit down with everyone who contributed to the research in this book so as to continue our conversations and plan future experiments. Sadly, obvious obstacles stand in the way. I must content myself with thanking all my students and collaborators whose creative and persistent engagement pushed me ever further on the path to discovery. I especially want to thank Marieke Adriaanse, Angela Lee Duckworth, Caterina Gawrilow, Heidi Grant Halvorson, Andreas Kappes, Heather Barry Kappes, Daniel Kirk, Michael K. Marquardt, Doris Mayer, Hyeon-ju Pak, Bettina Schwörer, A. Timur Sevincer, Gertraud Stadler, Mike Wendt, and Sandra Wittleder. Thank you as well to the undergraduate students whose hard work and devotion contributed so much to our research.

Many people gave of their time to participate in our studies. I am grateful to them as well as to the institutions and funding

189

agencies whose generosity made our research possible, among them the Max Planck Institute for Human Development in Berlin, the University of Hamburg, New York University, the Bill & Melinda Gates Foundation, the Deutsche Angestellten Krankenkasse (DAK Gesundheit), the German Research Foundation (DFG), the German Academic Exchange Service (DAAD), and the National Institutes of Health (NIH).

Ilaria Dagnini Brey, Scott J. Kieserman, and Klaus Michael Reininger read drafts of this book and offered essential suggestions. But this book would not exist at all had Brooke Carey at Portfolio not taken the initiative and convinced me to bring my findings to the world. Brooke introduced me to Adrian Zackheim and Emily Angell, both of whom generously and constructively guided me through the publication process. Margot Stamas's and Jesse Maeshiro's help was also invaluable. My agent, Giles Anderson, patiently supported me throughout, while my writing guru Seth Schulman helped a nonnative English speaker craft what I hope is a readable book. Seth made the entire process incredibly fun and enlightening. I will miss our sessions together and will always feel indebted to him for our wonderful collaboration.

Doris Mayer, my longtime collaborator and friend, supported me not only in revising this book but in completing numerous research studies. Bettina Schwörer gave me the courage to disseminate our research findings and provided invaluable help in the creation of the WOOP apps.

Finally, there is my family: My aunt Therese, with whom everything started; and my sons, Anton and Jakob, who stood by me throughout the many years of research. Peter, my husband and intellectual companion, always encouraged and supported my offbeat research ideas. I feel so blessed to share with him my present reality and my wishes for the future.

Notes

Chapter 1

1. Rhonda Byrne, *The Secret* (New York: Atria Books, 2006).
2. Jack Canfield, Mark V. Hansen, and Amy Newmark, *Chicken Soup for the Soul: Think Positive: 101 Inspirational Stories About Counting Your Blessings and Having a Positive Attitude* (Chicken Soup for the Soul Publishing, 2010).
3. Ibid., VIII.
4. Valdemar Galvan, *How to Think Positive: Get Out of the Hole of Negative Thinking and Find Your Ultimate Potential* (CreateSpace Independent Publishing Platform, 2012).
5. "From Pepsi Optimism Project (POP): Americans Believe Ideas from 'Regular People' Will Save the Day," PepsiCo, published January 11, 2010, accessed February 19, 2014, http://www.pepsico.com/PressRelease/From-Pepsi-Optimism-Project-POP-Americans-Believe-Ideas-from-Regular-People-Will01112010.html.
6. Michael De Groote, "Optimism and American Dream Surviving Pragmatism, Survey Shows," *Deseret News*, May 22, 2013, accessed February 19, 2014, http://www.deseretnews.com/article/765630382/Optimism-and-American-Dream-surviving-pragmatism-survey-shows.html?pg=all.
7. Frank Newport, "Americans Optimistic About Life in 2013: Democrats, Younger Adults Most Positive," *GALLUP Politics*, January 3, 2013, accessed February 19, 2014, http://www.gallup.com/poll/159698/americans-optimistic-life-2013.aspx.

Notes

8. Marcus Aurelius, *Meditations*, trans. Martin Hammond (London: Penguin Books Limited, 2006).

9. As quoted in Jabez (uncle), *Uncle Jabez; or The Teachings of Adversity* (London: The Religious Tract Society, 1799), 7, accessed February 21, 2014, http://books.google.de/books?id=aEUDAAAAQAAJ&printsec=frontcover&hl=de&source=gbs_ge_summary_r&redir_esc=y#v=onepage&q&f=false.

10. Dr. Seuss, *Oh, the Places You'll Go!* (New York: Random House, 1990).

11. Charles Chaplin, "Swing Little Girl," soundtrack of *The Circus*, 1968 © 1954 by Bourne Co.

12. Gabriele Oettingen et al., "Causality, Agency, and Control Beliefs in East Versus West Berlin Children: A Natural Experiment on the Role of Context," *Journal of Personality and Social Psychology* 66 (1994): 579–595; Gabriele Oettingen, "Cross-Cultural Perspectives on Self-Efficacy" in *Self-Efficacy in Changing Societies*, ed. Albert Bandura (New York: Cambridge University Press, 1995), 149–176.

13. Gabriele Oettingen and Martin E. P. Seligman, "Pessimism and Behavioral Signs of Depression in East Versus West Berlin," *European Journal of Social Psychology* 20 (1990): 207–220.

14. Martin E. P. Seligman, *Learned Optimism* (New York: Knopf, 1991).

15. Sigmund Freud, *On Psychopathology* (New York: Penguin Freud Library, 1993).

16. William James, *The Principles of Psychology*, vol. 2 (London: Macmillan, 1891), 283.

17. Albert Bandura, *Self-Efficacy: The Exercise of Control* (New York: Freeman, 1997).

18. Seligman, *Learned Optimism*.

19. This study is described in Gabriele Oettingen and Thomas A. Wadden, "Expectation, Fantasy, and Weight Loss: Is the Impact of Positive Thinking Always Positive?" *Cognitive Therapy and Research* 15 (1991): 167–175. I want to acknowledge the research contribution to this study of Thomas A. Wadden, who is the Albert J. Stunkard Professor of Psychology in Psychiatry, University of Pennsylvania. I also draw on Gabriele Oettingen, "Future Thought and Behaviour Change," *European Review of Social Psychology* 23 (2012): 1–63.

20. Text from this paragraph adapted without quotation from Gabriele Oettingen, "Future Thought and Behaviour Change."

21. This study and the next three studies are described in Gabriele Oettingen and Doris Mayer, "The Motivating Function of Thinking About the Future: Expectations Versus Fantasies," *Journal of Personality and Social Psychology* 83 (2002): 1198–1212. I want to acknowledge the research

contribution to this study of Anette Losert and Doris Mayer. Doris Mayer is a fellow researcher at the Center for Research on Motivation, University of Hamburg, Germany.

22. "Activities After Hip Replacement," American Academy of Orthopaedic Surgeons, OrthoInfo.org, accessed February 27, 2014, http://orthoinfo .aaos.org/topic.cfm?topic=a00356.

23. Heather Barry Kappes, Gabriele Oettingen, and Doris Mayer, "Positive Fantasies Predict Low Academic Achievement in Disadvantaged Students," *European Journal of Social Psychology* 42 (2012): 53–64.

24. Charles Gore, "The Global Recession of 2009 in a Long-Term Development Perspective," *Journal of International Development* 22 (2010): 714–738.

25. James W. Pennebaker et al., *The Development and Psychometric Properties of LIWC2007* (Austin, TX: LIWC.net, 2007).

26. This study and the next one are described in A. Timur Sevincer et al., "Positive Fantasies About the Future in Newspaper Reports and Presidential Addresses Predict Economic Downturn," *Psychological Science* 25 (2014): 1010–1017. A. Timur Sevincer is a former graduate student and now assistant professor at the Center for Research on Motivation, University of Hamburg. I also want to acknowledge the research contribution to this study of Greta Wagner and Johanna Kalvelage. Greta Wagner is a graduate student at the Center for Research on Motivation, University of Hamburg.

27. Nancy C. Lutkehaus, *Margaret Mead: The Making of an American Icon* (Princeton, NJ: Princeton University Press, 2008), 261.

28. Josep Isern, Mary C. Meaney, and Sarah Wilson, "Corporate Transformation Under Pressure," mckinseyquarterly.com, April 2009, accessed February 21, 2014, http://www.mckinsey.com/insights/organization/corporate_ transformation_under_pressure.

29. "Leaders of Change: Companies Prepare for a Stronger Future," *Report from the Economist Intelligence Unit*, 2011, accessed February 21, 2014, http://www.managementthinking.eiu.com/sites/default/files/downloads/ Celerant_LeadersOfChange_final%20final.pdf.

30. Mitch Ditkoff, "56 Reasons Why Most Corporate Innovation Initiatives Fail," Huffington Post, October 12, 2012, accessed February 21, 2014, http://www.huffingtonpost.com/mitch-ditkoff/post_3992_b_1960239 .html.

31. "Frequently Asked Questions About Small Business," SBA Office of Advocacy, September 2012, accessed February 21, 2014, http://www.sba.gov/ sites/default/files/FAQ_Sept_2012.pdf.

32. Steve Jacobs, chairman of the Continuous Learning Group, telephone interview, October 11, 2013.

Chapter 2

1. Sigmund Freud, *Introductory Lectures on Psycho-Analysis* (Penguin Freud Library 1, 1991, original work published 1915), 419.
2. Marie Jahoda, *Current Concepts of Positive Mental Health* (New York: Basic Books, 1958), 49.
3. Abraham H. Maslow, "Self-Actualizing People: A Study of Psychological Health," *Personality Symposia: Symposium No. 1 on Values* (1950): 11–34.
4. As a caveat, it's worth noting that humanistic psychologists, Neo-Freudians, and Freudians didn't necessarily focus on fantasies per se but rather on "illusions," which were thought of as a way to escape "reality." This book, by contrast, is about fantasies about the future, defined as free thoughts and images about future events and scenarios. Fantasies in this view bear no inherent relation to how real or unreal a remembered or anticipated event or scenario may be. They are just thoughts about an event rather than judgments as to whether an event has happened in the past or will happen in the future.
5. Barbara Ehrenreich, *Bright Sided: How the Relentless Promotion of Positive Thinking Has Undermined America* (New York: Henry Holt, 2009), 196.
6. Rabbi Charles Sherman, telephone interview by Seth Schulman, Syracuse, New York, August 8, 2013.
7. Martin Luther King Jr., "I Have a Dream" (speech, Washington, DC, August 28, 1963), American Rhetoric, accessed February 27, 2014, http://www.americanrhetoric.com/speeches/mlkihaveadream.htm.
8. Quoted in Dr. Myrna Goldenberg, "Cookbooks and Concentration Camps: Unlikely Partners." Jewish Virtual Library, accessed February 21, 2014, http://www.jewishvirtuallibrary.org/jsource/Holocaust/cookbook.html.
9. Michael Berenbaum, foreward to *In Memory's Kitchen: A Legacy from the Women of Terezin*, ed. Cara DeSilva (Lanham, MD: Rowman & Littlefield, 2006), XVI.
10. Eugenia Halsey, "Relatives Treasure Recipes Left by Holocaust Victims," CNN.com, October 24, 1996, accessed February 21, 2014, http://edition.cnn.com/WORLD/9610/24/holocaust.memories/index.html.
11. This study and the three that follow are described in Heather Barry Kappes, Bettina Schwörer, and Gabriele Oettingen, "Needs Instigate Positive Fantasies of Idealized Futures," *European Journal of Social Psychology* 42 (2012): 299–307. Heather Barry Kappes is a former graduate student of the Motivation Lab at New York University that I coteach with my husband, Peter M. Gollwitzer, professor of psychology at New York University. She is now a lecturer of marketing at the London School of Economics and

Political Science. I also want to acknowledge the research contribution to these studies of Bettina Schwörer, a graduate student at the Center for Research on Motivation, University of Hamburg.

12. Abraham H. Maslow, "A Theory of Human Motivation," *Psychological Review* 50 (1943): 370–396.

13. Edward L. Deci and Richard M. Ryan, "The 'What' and 'Why' of Goal Pursuits: Human Needs and the Self-Determination of Behavior," *Psychological Inquiry* 11, (2000): 227–268.

14. William James, *Psychology: Briefer Course* (New York: Henry Holt & Co., 1920), 448.

15. Rabbi Charles Sherman, telephone interview by Seth Schulman, Syracuse, New York, August 8, 2013.

16. Mary Beth Williams and Soili Poijula, *The PTSD Workbook: Simple, Effective Techniques for Overcoming Traumatic Stress Symptoms*, 2nd ed. (Oakland, CA: New Harbinger Publications, 2013).

17. Gallup, "State of the American Workplace: Employee Engagement Insights for U.S. Business Leaders," Gallup.com, accessed February 22, 2014, http://www.gallup.com/file/strategicconsulting/163007/State%20of%20the%20American%20Workplace%20Report%202013.pdf.

18. Jerome L. Singer, *Daydreaming* (New York: Random House, 1966).

19. Eric Klinger, "Consequences of Commitment to and Disengagement from Incentives," *Psychological Review* 82 (1975): 1–25.

20. American College Health Association, "American College Health Association—National College Health Assessment II: Reference Group Executive Summary Spring 2013" (Hanover, MD: American College Health Association, 2013), accessed February 28, 2014, http://www.acha-ncha.org/docs/ACHA-NCHA-II_ReferenceGroup_ExecutiveSummary_Spring2013.pdf.

21. This study is described in Gabriele Oettingen, Doris Mayer, and Sam Portnow, "Positive Fantasies About the Future Predict Depressive Symptoms," manuscript under revision. I want to acknowledge the research contribution to this study of Sam Portnow.

22. Inge Seiffge-Krenke and Nicolai Klessinger, "Long-Term Effects of Avoidant Coping on Adolescents' Depressive Symptoms," *Journal of Youth and Adolescence* 29 (2000): 617–630.

Chapter 3

1. This study is described in Heather Barry Kappes and Gabriele Oettingen, "Positive Fantasies About Idealized Futures Sap Energy," *Journal of Experimental Social Psychology* 47 (2011): 719–729.

2. Rex A. Wright and Leslie D. Kirby, "Effort Determination of Cardiovascular Response: An Integrative Analysis with Applications in Social Psychology," in *Advances in Experimental Social Psychology*, ed. Mark P. Zanna (San Diego, CA: Academic Press, 2001), 33: 255–307.

3. Kimberly A. Brownley, Barry E. Hurwitz, and Neil Schneiderman, "Cardiovascular Psychophysiology," in *Handbook of Psychophysiology*, 2nd ed., ed. John T. Cacioppo, Louis G. Tassinary, and Gary G. Berntson (New York: Cambridge University Press, 2000), 224–264.

4. "How Do Alcohol, Coffee, and Smoking Influence Blood Pressure?" MedicineNet.com, August 8, 2002, accessed February 22, 2014, http://www.medicinenet.com/script/main/art.asp?articlekey=20340.

5. This study and the next one are described in Heather Barry Kappes, Eesha Sharma, and Gabriele Oettingen, "Positive Fantasies Dampen Charitable Giving When Many Resources Are Demanded," *Journal of Consumer Psychology* 23 (2013): 128–135. I want to acknowledge the research contribution to these studies of Eesha Sharma, a former graduate student at the Leonard N. Stern School of Business, New York University. She is now assistant professor of business administration, Tuck School of Business at Dartmouth University.

6. Caryl M. Stern, *I Believe in ZERO: Learning from the World's Children* (New York: St. Martin's Press, 2013).

7. Utpal M. Dholakia, "How Businesses Fare with Daily Deals: A Multi-Site Analysis of Groupon, Livingsocial, Opentable, Travelzoo, and BuyWithMe Promotions (June 13, 2011)," Rice University—Jesse H. Jones Graduate School of Business, accessed March 3, 2014, http://dx.doi.org/10.2139/ssrn.1863466.

8. This study and the next one are described in Kappes and Oettingen, "Positive Fantasies About Idealized Futures Sap Energy."

9. David Hume, *A Treatise of Human Nature, Vol. 1 of the Understanding* (London: John Noon, 1739).

10. Jean Decety et al., "Vegetative Response During Imagined Movement Is Proportional to Mental Effort," *Behavioural Brain Research* 42 (1991): 1–5; Eric Klinger, *Structure and Functions of Fantasy* (Oxford: Wiley-Interscience, 1971); Eric Klinger, "The Nature of Fantasy and Its Clinical Uses," *Psychotherapy: Theory, Research & Practice* 14 (1977): 223–231; David C. McClelland, "Longitudinal Trends in the Relation of Thought to Action," *Journal of Consulting Psychology* 30 (1966): 479–483; C. E. McMahon, "Images as Motives and Motivators: A Historical Perspective," *American Journal of Psychology* 86 (1973): 465–490.

11. Carey K. Morewedge, Young Eun Huh, and Joachim Vosgerau, "Thought for Food: Imagined Consumption Reduces Actual Consumption," *Science* 330 (2010): 1530–1533.

12. This study is described in Heather Barry Kappes, Andreas Kappes, and Gabriele Oettingen, "When Attainment Is All in Your Head," unpublished paper. Andreas Kappes is a former graduate student at the Center for Research on Motivation, University of Hamburg. He is now a postdoctoral fellow at the University College London.

13. Markus Denzler, Jens Förster, and Nira Liberman, "How Goal-Fulfillment Decreases Aggression," *Journal of Experimental Social Psychology* 45 (2009): 90–100; Richard L. Marsh, Jason L. Hicks, and Martin L. Bink, "Activation of Completed, Uncompleted, and Partially Completed Intentions," *Journal of Experimental Psychology: Learning, Memory, and Cognition* 24 (1998): 350–361.

14. This study is described in Heather Barry Kappes and Gabriele Oettingen, "Wishful Information Preference: Positive Fantasies Mimic the Effects of Intentions," *Personality and Social Psychology Bulletin* 38 (2012): 870–881.

15. "Pump bump" is a hard little bump that forms on the back of the heel where the strap touches the skin.

Chapter 4

1. Wright and Kirby, "Effort Determination of Cardiovascular Response."

2. William James, *The Principles of Psychology*, vol. 1 (London: Macmillan, 1890), 239.

3. This study is described in Gabriele Oettingen, Hyeon-ju Pak, and Karoline Schnetter, "Self-Regulation of Goal Setting: Turning Free Fantasies About the Future into Binding Goals," *Journal of Personality and Social Psychology* 80 (2001): 736–753. I want to acknowledge the research contribution to these studies of Hyeon-ju Pak, Karoline Schnetter, and Anette Losert. Hyeon-ju Pak is a former postdoctoral fellow at the Center for Research on Motivation, University of Hamburg.

4. This study is described in Gabriele Oettingen, "Expectancy Effects on Behavior Depend on Self-Regulatory Thought," *Social Cognition* 18 (2000): 101–129. I want to acknowledge the research contribution to this study of Birgit Böhringer.

5. This study is described in Gabriele Oettingen et al., "Mental Contrasting and Goal Commitment: The Mediating Role of Energization," *Personality*

and Social Psychology Bulletin 35 (2009): 608–622. I want to acknowledge the research contribution to this study of Doris Mayer, Elisabeth J. Stephens, Hyeon-ju Pak, and Meike Hagenah.

6. This research is described in A. Timur Sevincer and Gabriele Oettingen, "Future Thought and the Self-Regulation of Energization," in *Handbook of Biobehavioral Approaches to Self-Regulation*, ed. G. H. E. Gendolla, M. Tops, and S. Koole (New York: Springer, in press).

7. This study is described in Oettingen, Pak, and Schnetter, "Self-Regulation of Goal Setting: Turning Free Fantasies About the Future into Binding Goals."

8. Arie Nadler and Jeffrey D. Fisher, "The Role of Threat to Self Esteem and Perceived Control in Recipient Reactions to Aid: Theory Development and Empirical Validation," in *Advances in Experimental Social Psychology* (vol. 19), ed. L. Berkowitz (New York: Academic Press, 1986), 81–124.

9. National Pharmacy Association, "An Interim Review by the National Pharmacy Association of Men's Uptake of Pharmacy Services (November 2012)," npa.co.uk, accessed March 3, 2014, http://www.npa.co.uk/Documents/Docstore/AYP2012/AN_INTERIM_REVIEW_BY_THE_NPA_OF_MEN%E2%80%99S_UPTAKE_OF_PHARMACY_SERVICES_NOVEMBER%202012_.pdf.

10. Jamie Doward, "Men Risk Health by Failing to Seek NHS Help, Survey Finds," *The Observer* [UK], November 3, 2012, accessed February 23, 2014, http://www.theguardian.com/society/2012/nov/04/men-failing-seek-nhs-help.

11. Justin Hunt and Daniel Eisenberg, "Mental Health Problems and Help-Seeking Behavior Among College Students," *Journal of Adolescent Health* 46 (2010): 3–10.

12. Christy M. Walcott and Ajlana Music, "Promoting Adolescent Help-Seeking for Mental-Health Problems: Strategies for School-Based Professionals," *Communique* 41, issue 1 (September 2012): 6–7; see also Marieke Zwaanswijk et al., "Help Seeking for Emotional and Behavioural Problems in Children and Adolescents: A Review of Recent Literature," *European Child & Adolescent Psychiatry* 12 (2003): 153–161.

13. Kimberly A. Schonert-Reichl, Daniel Offer, and Kenneth I. Howard, "Seeking Help from Informal and Formal Resources During Adolescence: Sociodemographic and Psychological Correlates," *Adolescent Psychiatry* 20 (1995): 165–178.

14. Katie Schuck, "Can't Ask for Help," huffingtonpost.com, August 28, 2012, accessed February 23, 2014, http://www.huffingtonpost.com/ct-working-moms/asking-for-help_b_1821559.html.

15. Danielle Rondeau, "It's Not OK, I'm Not Fine, I Can't Do Life Alone—Why the Reasons We Don't Ask for Help Just Aren't Good Enough!" Trash Your Stress, accessed September 18, 2013, http://trashyourstress.com/2013/05/12/its-not-ok-im-not-fine-i-cant-do-life-alone-why-the-reasons-we-dont-ask-for-help-just-arent-good-enough/.

16. This study is described in Gabriele Oettingen et al., "Mental Contrasting and the Self-Regulation of Helping Relations," *Social Cognition* 28 (2010): 490–508. I want to acknowledge the research contribution to these studies of Elizabeth J. Stephens, Doris Mayer, Linda Schmidt, and Babette Brinkmann. Babette Brinkmann is a former graduate student at the University of Heidelberg, Germany.

17. Albert Bandura, "Self-Efficacy: Toward a Unifying Theory of Behavioral Change," *Psychological Review* 84 (1977): 191–215.

18. Barbara J. Lombardo and Daniel J. Roddy, "Cultivating Organizational Creativity in an Age of Complexity: A Companion Study to the IBM 2010 Global Chief Human Resource Officer Study," IBM Institute for Business Value, accessed March 3, 2014, http://www-935.ibm.com/services/us/gbs/thoughtleadership/ibv-organizational-creativity.html.

19. Gene D. Cohen, "Research of Creativity and Aging: The Positive Impact of the Arts on Health and Illness," *Generations* 30 (2006): 7–15; Nicholas A. Turiano, Avron Spiro III, and Daniel K. Mroczek, "Openness to Experience and Mortality in Men: Analysis of Trait and Facets," *Journal of Aging and Health* 24 (2012): 654–672.

20. This study and the following one are described in Gabriele Oettingen, Michael K. Marquardt, and Peter M. Gollwitzer, "Mental Contrasting Turns Positive Feedback on Creative Potential into Successful Performance," *Journal of Experimental Social Psychology* 48 (2012): 990–996. I want to acknowledge the research contribution to these studies of Michael K. Marquardt and Peter M. Gollwitzer. Michael K. Marquardt is a former graduate student at the University of Konstanz, Germany, and Peter M. Gollwitzer is professor of psychology at New York University and at the University of Konstanz.

21. Harrison G. Gough, "A Creative Personality Scale for the Adjective Check List," *Journal of Personality and Social Psychology* 37 (1979): 1398–1405.

22. The answer to this problem is as follows: Put nine animals in each of three small pens. Then build a larger pen enclosing the three smaller ones. The smaller pens each have an odd number of animals in them (nine in each) and the large pen has a total of twenty-seven animals enclosed within it.

23. Bernd Baumgartl and Adrian Favell, *New Xenophobia in Europe* (London: Kluwer Law International, 1995).

24. This study is described in Gabriele Oettingen et al., "Turning Fantasies About Positive and Negative Futures into Self-Improvement Goals," *Motivation and Emotion* 29 (2005): 237–267. I want to acknowledge the research contribution to this study of Doris Mayer, Jennifer S. Thorpe, Hanna Janetzke, and Solvig Lorenz. Jennifer S. Thorpe is a former graduate student in the Psychology Department of New York University.
25. Michael W. Eysenck, *Anxiety: The Cognitive Perspective* (London: Erlbaum, 1992); Donald O. Hebb, "Drives and the C.N.S. (Conceptual Nervous System)," *Psychological Review* 62 (1955): 243-254.

Chapter 5

1. Karol M. Wasylyshyn, "Executive Coaching: An Outcome Study," *Consulting Psychology Journal: Practice and Research* 55 (2003): 94–106.
2. In using the word "perception," I'm referring to how people generally make sense of reality, not to how they organize, identify, and interpret sensory information (Daniel L. Schacter, Daniel T. Gilbert, and Daniel M. Wegner, *Psychology* [New York: Worth Publishers, 2010]). In scholarly work, psychologists tend to use perception in the latter, narrower sense.
3. This and the next study are described in Andreas Kappes and Gabriele Oettingen, "The Emergence of Goal Pursuit: Mental Contrasting Connects Future and Reality," *Journal of Experimental Social Psychology* 54 (2014): 25–39.
4. Adriaan Spruyt, Anne Gast, and Agnes Moors, "The Sequential Priming Paradigm: A Primer," in *Cognitive Methods in Social Psychology*, eds. Karl Christoph Klauer, Andreas Voss, and Christoph Stahl (New York: Guilford Press, 2011), 48–77.
5. We interspersed these control trials and the experimental trials with other control trials in which we used irrelevant positive and negative words as primes (e.g., "friendly," "corruption") and with dozens of "filler" trials that contained only neutral words (e.g., "umbrella," "noon").
6. This study is described in Andreas Kappes, Henrik Singmann, and Gabriele Oettingen, "Mental Contrasting Instigates Goal Pursuit by Linking Obstacles of Reality with Instrumental Behavior," *Journal of Experimental Social Psychology* 48 (2012): 811–818. I want to acknowledge the research contribution to this study of Henrik Singmann.
7. This study and the two that follow are described in Andreas Kappes et al., "Mental Contrasting Changes the Meaning of Reality," *Journal of Experimental Social Psychology* 49 (2013): 797–810. I want to acknowledge the

research contribution to these studies of Mike Wendt and Tilman Reinelt. Mike Wendt is a former professor of cognitive psychology at the University of Hamburg and now at the Helmut Schmidt University, Hamburg.

8. Andrea Kiesel et al., "Control and Compatibility in Task Switching—A Review," *Psychological Bulletin* 136 (2010): 849–874.

9. As a reward for their participation, all children received a special certificate, and nine winners of the lottery received a computer game.

10. John Hattie and Helen Timperley, "The Power of Feedback," *Review of Educational Research* 77 (2007): 81–112.

11. Constantine Sedikides and Jeffrey D. Green, "Memory as a Self-Protective Mechanism," *Social and Personality Psychology Compass* 3 (2009): 1055–1068.

12. This study and the two that follow are described in Andreas Kappes, Gabriele Oettingen, and Hyeon-ju Pak, "Mental Contrasting and the Self-Regulation of Responding to Negative Feedback," *Personality and Social Psychology Bulletin* 38 (2012): 845–856. I want to acknowledge the research contribution to these studies of Andreas Kappes and Hyeon-ju Pak.

13. Henry A. Murray, *Explorations in Personality* (New York: Oxford University Press, 1938).

Chapter 6

1. John H. Flavell, "Metacognition and Cognitive Monitoring: A New Area of Cognitive-Developmental Inquiry," *American Psychologist* 34 (1979): 906–911; John H. Flavell, "Theory-of-Mind Development: Retrospect and Prospect," *Merrill-Palmer Quarterly* 50 (2004): 274–290.

2. This study is described in Gabriele Oettingen, Doris Mayer, and Babette Brinkmann, "Mental Contrasting of Future and Reality: Managing the Demands of Everyday Life in Health Care Professionals," *Journal of Personnel Psychology* 9 (2010): 138–144. I want to acknowledge the research contribution to this study of Doris Mayer and Babette Brinkmann.

3. In this and the other studies in which we tested mental contrasting as an intervention, we also offered mental contrasting to members of control groups after the study was concluded.

4. This study and the next study mentioned are described in Anton Gollwitzer et al., "Mental Contrasting Facilitates Academic Performance in School Children," *Motivation and Emotion* 35 (2011): 403–412. Anton Gollwitzer is an undergraduate psychology major at New York University. I also want to acknowledge the research contribution to this study of Teri

A. Kirby, Angela L. Duckworth, and Doris Mayer. Teri A. Kirby is a graduate student in the Department of Psychology, University of Washington in Seattle. Angela L. Duckworth is associate professor in the Department of Psychology, University of Pennsylvania, Philadelphia.

5. These studies are described in A. Timur Sevincer, P. Daniel Busatta, and Gabriele Oettingen, "Mental Contrasting and Transfer of Energization," *Personality and Social Psychology Bulletin* 40 (2014): 139–152. I want to acknowledge the research contribution to this study of A. Timur Sevincer and P. Daniel Busatta.

6. This account of implementation intentions is described in Peter M. Gollwitzer, "Implementation Intentions: Strong Effects of Simple Plans," *American Psychologist* 54 (1999): 493–503.

7. Thomas L. Webb and Paschal Sheeran, "Does Changing Behavioral Intentions Engender Behavior Change? A Meta-Analysis of the Experimental Evidence," *Psychological Bulletin* 132 (2006): 249–268.

8. This study is described in Peter M. Gollwitzer and Veronika Brandstätter, "Implementation Intentions and Effective Goal Pursuit," *Journal of Personality and Social Psychology* 73 (1997): 186–199. Veronika Brandstätter is a former graduate student at the Max Planck Institute for Psychological Research in Munich, Germany. She is now professor of psychology at the University of Zurich, Switzerland.

9. Peter M. Gollwitzer and Paschal Sheeran, "Implementation Intentions and Goal Achievement: A Meta-Analysis of Effects and Processes," *Advances in Experimental Psychology* 38 (2006): 69–119.

10. Veronika Brandstätter, Angelika Lengfelder, and Peter M. Gollwitzer, "Implementation Intentions and Efficient Action Initiation," *Journal of Personality and Social Psychology* 81 (2001): 946–960.

11. Peter M. Gollwitzer and Gabriele Oettingen, "Planning Promotes Goal Striving," in *Handbook of Self-Regulation: Research, Theory, and Applications*, eds. K. D. Vohs and R. F. Baumeister (New York: Guilford Press, 2011), 162–185.

12. Paschal Sheeran, Thomas L. Webb, and Peter M. Gollwitzer, "The Interplay Between Goal Intentions and Implementation Intentions," *Personality and Social Psychology Bulletin* 31 (2005): 87–98.

13. This study is described in Marieke A. Adriaanse et al., "When Planning Is Not Enough: Fighting Unhealthy Snacking Habits by Mental Contrasting with Implementation Intentions (MCII)," *European Journal of Social Psychology* 40 (2010): 1277–1293. Marieke A. Adriaanse is assistant professor at the Self-Regulation Lab, Utrecht University, the Netherlands. I also

want to acknowledge the research contribution to this study of Peter M. Gollwitzer, Erin P. Hennes, Denise T. D. De Ridder, and John B. F. De Wit. Erin P. Hennes is a former graduate student in the Psychology Department, New York University, and now postdoctoral fellow at the Psychology of Social Justice Lab, University of California, Los Angeles. Denise T. D. De Ridder is director of the Self-Regulation Lab, Utrecht University. John B. F. De Wit is professor at the Centre for Social Research in Health, University of New South Wales, Sydney, Australia.

Chapter 7

1. The studies mentioned in this paragraph are described in A. Timur Sevincer and Gabriele Oettingen, "Spontaneous Mental Contrasting and Selective Goal Pursuit," *Personality and Social Psychology Bulletin* 39 (2013): 1240–1254.
2. Relevant studies are described in Heather Barry Kappes et al., "Sad Mood Promotes Self-Initiated Mental Contrasting of Future and Reality," *Emotion* 11 (2011): 1206–1222. I want to acknowledge the research contribution to these studies of Heather Barry Kappes, Sam Maglio, and Doris Mayer. Sam Maglio is a former graduate student in the Psychology Department, New York University; he is now assistant professor of marketing, University of Toronto, Scarborough, Canada.
3. This study is described in Anja Achtziger et al., "Strategies of Intention Formation Are Reflected in Continuous MEG Activity," *Social Neuroscience* 4 (2009): 11–27. I want to acknowledge the research contribution to this study of Anja Achtziger, Thorsten Fehr, Peter M. Gollwitzer, and Brigitte Rockstroh. Anja Achtziger is professor of psychology, Zeppelin University, Friedrichshafen, Germany; Thorsten Fehr is senior scientist at the University of Bremen, Germany; Brigitte Rockstroh is professor of clinical psychology, University of Konstanz.
4. "Chronic Diseases: The Power to Prevent, the Call to Control," National Center for Chronic Disease Prevention and Health Promotion, 2009, accessed February 24, 2014, http://www.cdc.gov/chronicdisease/resources/publications/aag/pdf/chronic.pdf.
5. Kenneth D. Kochanek et al., "Deaths: Final Data for 2009," *National Vital Statistics Reports* 60 (2011): 1–117, accessed February 24, 2014, http://www.cdc.gov/nchs/data/nvsr/nvsr60/nvsr60_03.pdf; Paul A. Heidenreich et al., "Forecasting the Future of Cardiovascular Disease in the United States: A Policy Statement from the American Heart Association," *Circulation* 123 (2011): 933–944.

6. Rod K. Dishman, "Increasing and Maintaining Exercise and Physical Activity," *Behaviour Therapy* 22 (1991): 345–378, as cited in Gabriele Oettingen, "Future Thought and Behaviour Change," *European Review of Social Psychology* 23 (2012), 1–63.

7. I want to thank Frau Hella Thomas for her very constructive collaboration.

8. This study is described in Gertraud Stadler, Gabriele Oettingen, and Peter M. Gollwitzer, "Physical Activity in Women: Effects of a Self-Regulation Intervention," *American Journal of Preventative Medicine* 36 (2009): 29–34; Gertraud Stadler, Gabriele Oettingen, and Peter M. Gollwitzer, "Intervention Effects of Information and Self-Regulation on Eating Fruits and Vegetables over Two Years," *Health Psychology* 29 (2010): 274–283. Gertraud Stadler is a former graduate student at the Center for Research on Motivation, University of Hamburg, and now associate research scientist at Columbia University.

9. Ronald W. Rogers, "Cognitive and Physiological Processes in Fear Appeals and Attitude Change: A Revised Theory of Protection Motivation," in *Social Psychophysiology: A Sourcebook*, ed. J. Cacioppo and R. Petty (New York: Guilford Press, 1983), 153–176.

10. Albert Bandura, "Human Agency in Social Cognitive Theory," *American Psychologist* 44 (1989): 1175–1184; Albert Bandura, "Self-Efficacy: Toward a Unifying Theory of Behavioral Change."

11. Martin Fishbein and Icek Ajzen, *Belief, Attitude, Intention, and Behavior: An Introduction to Theory and Research* (Reading, MA: Addison-Wesley, 1975).

12. Icek Ajzen, "The Theory of Planned Behavior," *Organizational Behavior and Human Decision Processes* 50 (1991): 179–211.

13. Edward C. Tolman, *Purposive Behavior in Animals and Men* (New York: Appleton-Century, 1932).

14. Susan Michie et al., "Effective Techniques in Healthy Eating and Physical Activity Interventions: A Meta-Regression," *Health Psychology* 28 (2009): 690–701, cited in Paschal Sheeran et al., "Gone Exercising: Mental Contrasting Promotes Physical Activity Among Overweight, Middle-Aged, Low SES Fishermen," *Health Psychology* 32 (2013): 802–809.

15. Deborah A. Prentice and Dale T. Miller, "Pluralistic Ignorance and Alcohol Use on Campus: Some Consequences of Misperceiving the Social Norm," *Journal of Personality and Social Psychology* 64 (1993): 243–256.

16. William R. Miller, "Motivation for Treatment: A Review with Special Emphasis on Alcoholism," *Psychological Bulletin* 98 (1985): 84–107.

17. Carol S. Dweck and Ellen L. Leggett, "A Social-Cognitive Approach to Motivation and Personality," *Psychological Review* 95 (1988): 256–273;

Carol S. Dweck, *Mindset: The New Psychology of Success* (New York: Random House, 2006).

18. Edwin A. Locke and Gary P. Latham, *A Theory of Goal Setting and Task Performance* (Englewood Cliffs, NJ: Prentice Hall, 1990); Edwin A. Locke and Gary P. Latham, *New Developments in Goal Setting and Task Performance* (New York: Routledge, 2013).

19. This study is described in Sandra Christiansen et al., "A Short Goal-Pursuit Intervention to Improve Physical Capacity: A Randomized Clinical Trial in Chronic Back Pain Patients," *Pain* 149 (2010): 444–452. I want to acknowledge the research contribution to this study of Sandra Christiansen, Bernhard Dahme, and Regine Klinger, who are a former graduate student, professor (ret.), and senior research scientist, respectively, of clinical psychology at the University of Hamburg.

20. This study is described in Michael K. Marquardt et al., "Improving the Prevention of Secondary Strokes by the Self-Regulation Strategy of MCII: Stroke Patients' Physical Activity After One Year," submitted for publication. I want to acknowledge the research contribution to this study of Michael K. Marquardt, Peter M. Gollwitzer, and Joachim Liepert. Joachim Liepert is professor of medicine, Kliniken Schmieder, Allensbach, Germany.

21. Centers for Disease Control and Prevention, "Annual Smoking-Attributable Mortality, Years of Potential Life Lost, and Economic Costs—United States, 1995–1999," *Morbidity and Mortality Weekly Report* 51 (2002): 300–303, accessed June 5, 2013, http://www.cdc.gov/mmwr/preview/mmwrhtml/mm5114a2.htm.

22. "Alcohol Use and Health," Centers for Disease Control and Prevention (CDC), accessed June 5, 2013, http://www.cdc.gov/alcohol/fact-sheets/alcohol-use.htm.

23. Ralph W. Hingson et al., "Magnitude of Alcohol-Related Mortality and Morbidity Among U.S. College Students Ages 18–24," *Journal of Studies on Alcohol* 63 (2002): 136–144.

24. This study is described in Gabriele Oettingen et al., "Mental Contrasting with Implementation Intentions (MCII) Supports College Students in Regulating Their Alcohol Consumption" (presentation given at the meeting of the Society of Experimental Social Psychology, Austin, TX, October 27, 2012). I want to acknowledge the research contribution to this study of Sandra Wittleder, Andreas Kappes, Peter M. Gollwitzer, and Jon Morgenstern. Sandra Wittleder is a graduate student at the Center for Research on Motivation, University of Hamburg. Jon Morgenstern is professor of clinical psychology (in psychiatry), Columbia University.

25. This study is described in Sylviane Houssais, Gabriele Oettingen, and Doris Mayer, "Using Mental Contrasting with Implementation Intentions to Self-Regulate Insecurity-Based Behaviors in Relationships," *Motivation and Emotion* 37 (2013): 224–233. I want to acknowledge the research contribution to this study of Sylviane Houssais and Doris Mayer. Sylviane Houssais is a former graduate student in the Psychology Department at New York University.

26. Walter Mischel and Charlotte J. Patterson, "Effective Plans for Self-Control in Children," in *Minnesota Symposium on Child Psychology*, ed. W. A. Collins (Hillsdale, NJ: Erlbaum, 1978), 11:199–230; Inge Schweiger Gallo et al., "Strategic Automation of Emotion Regulation," *Journal of Personality and Social Psychology* 96 (2009): 11–31.

27. This study is described in Angela L. Duckworth et al., "Self-Regulation Strategies Improve Self-Discipline in Adolescents: Benefits of Mental Contrasting and Implementation Intentions," *Educational Psychology* 31 (2011): 17–26. I want to acknowledge the research contribution to this study of Heidi Grant Halverson, Benjamin Loew, and Peter M. Gollwitzer. Heidi Grant Halverson, a former postdoctoral student in the Motivation Lab at New York University, is associate director of the Motivation Science Center at Columbia Business School.

28. This study is described in Caterina Gawrilow et al., "Mental Contrasting with Implementation Intentions Enhances Self-Regulation of Goal Pursuit in Schoolchildren at Risk for ADHD," *Motivation and Emotion* 37 (2013): 134–145. I want to acknowledge the research contribution to this study of Caterina Gawrilow, Katrin Morgenroth, Regina Schultz, and Peter M. Gollwitzer. Caterina Gawrilow, a former postdoctoral student at the Center for Research on Motivation, University of Hamburg, is now professor of educational psychology at the University of Tübingen, Germany.

29. This study is described in Angela L. Duckworth et al., "From Fantasy to Action: Mental Contrasting with Implementation Intentions (MCII) Improves Academic Performance in Children. *Social Psychological and Personality Science* 4 (2013): 745–753. I want to acknowledge the research contribution to this study of Angela L. Duckworth, Teri A. Kirby, and Anton Gollwitzer.

30. This study is described in Gabriele Oettingen, Peter M. Gollwitzer, and Doris Mayer, "Mental Contrasting with Implementation Intentions (MCII) and Stress Coping," in preparation. I want to acknowledge the research contribution to this study of Christine E. Grund, Peter M. Gollwitzer, and Doris Mayer.

Chapter 8

1. Judith A. Ouellette and Wendy Wood, "Habit and Intention in Everyday Life: The Multiple Processes by Which Past Behavior Predicts Future Behavior," *Psychological Bulletin* 124 (1998): 54–74.

2. I am deeply indebted to Bettina Schwörer for her creativity, exceptional skills, and endless support in making the WOOP apps possible.

3. With funding from the Bill & Melinda Gates Foundation and the support of the College Knowledge Challenge Fund. I am most grateful to Keith W. Frome, cofounder of College Summit and founding headmaster of King Center Charter School, for his outstanding encouragement as we created the wooptoandthroughcollege app. I also want to thank Sean Murray, former project leader of CKC, for his outstanding guidance. Finally, I am indebted to Sally Marshall, senior corporate and foundation relations officer at New York University, for her prompt help in drafting the proposal.

4. Daniel Solórzano et al., "Pathways to Postsecondary Success Maximizing Opportunities for Youth in Poverty," pathways.gseis.ucla.edu, October 2013, accessed March 18, 2014, http://pathways.gseis.ucla.edu/publications/PathwaysReport.pdf; Michael N. Bastedo and Ozan Jaquette, "Running in Place: Low-Income Students and the Dynamics of Higher Education Stratification," *Educational Evaluation and Policy Analysis* 33 (2011): 318–339.

5. Keith W. Frome, e-mail message to author, September 30, 2013. I want to thank Keith W. Frome for sharing this event with me.

Credits

Figure 1

Sevincer, Wagner, Kalvelage, & Oettingen, "Positive Thinking About the Future in Newspaper Reports and Presidential Addresses Predicts Economic Downturn," *Psychological Science, 25,* 1010–1017, 2014, SAGE Journals.

Figure 2

Oettingen, Pak, & Schnetter, "Self-Regulation of Goal Setting: Turning Free Fantasies About the Future into Binding Goals," *Journal of Personality and Social Psychology, 80,* 736–753, 2001, American Psychological Association, adapted with permission.

Figure 3

Oettingen, "Expectancy Effects on Behavior Depend on Self-Regulatory Thought," *Social Cognition, 18,* 101–129, 2000.

© Guilford Press. Reprinted with permission from Guilford Press.

Figure 4

Oettingen, Mayer, Thorpe, Janetzke, & Lorenz, "Turning Fantasies About Positive and Negative Futures into Self-Improvement Goals," *Motivation and Emotion*, 29, 237–267, 2005, Springer Publishing Company.

Figure 6

A. Kappes & Oettingen, "The Emergence of Goal Pursuit: Mental Contrasting Connects Future and Reality," *Journal of Experimental Social Psychology*, 54, 25–39, 2014, American Psychological Association, adapted with permission.

Figure 7

A. Kappes, Singmann, & Oettingen, "Mental Contrasting Instigates Goal Pursuit by Linking Obstacles of Reality with Instrumental Behavior," *Journal of Experimental Social Psychology*, 48, 811–818, 2012, American Psychological Association, adapted with permission.

Figure 8

A. Kappes, Wendt, Reinelt, & Oettingen, "Mental Contrasting Changes the Meaning of Reality," *Journal of Experimental Social Psychology*, 49, 797–810, 2013, American Psychological Association, adapted with permission.

Figure 10

A. Kappes, Oettingen, & Pak, "Mental Contrasting and the Self-Regulation of Responding to Negative Feedback," *Personality and Social Psychology Bulletin, 38, 845–857*, 2012, SAGE Journals.

Figure 11

Adriaanse, Oettingen, Gollwitzer, Hennes, de Ridder, & de Wit, "When Planning Is Not Enough: Fighting Unhealthy Snacking Habits by Mental Contrasting with Implementation Intentions (MCII)," *European Journal of Social Psychology, 40, 1277–1293*, 2010, John Wiley & Sons, Inc.

Figure 12

Oettingen, "Future Thought and Behaviour Change," *European Review of Social Psychology, 23, 1–63*, 2012, Taylor & Francis.

Figure 13

Oettingen, "Future Thought and Behaviour Change," *European Review of Social Psychology, 23, 1–63*, 2012, Taylor & Francis.

Figure 14

Stadler, Oettingen, & Gollwitzer, "Physical Activity in Women: Effects of a Self-Regulation Intervention," *American Journal of Preventive Medicine, 36, 29–34*, 2009, Elsevier Inc.

Figure 15

Stadler, Oettingen, & Gollwitzer, "Intervention Effects of Information and Self-Regulation on Eating Fruits and Vegetables Over Two Years," *Health Psychology*, 29, 274–283, 2010, American Psychological Association, adapted with permission.

Figure 16

Oettingen, "Future Thought and Behaviour Change," *European Review of Social Psychology*, 23, 1–63, 2012, Taylor & Francis.

Index

Index

Index

Index